THE MESSENGERS

Francisco Cândido Xavier

THE MESSENGERS

(A mediumistic work)

When the worker is ready,
work will appear

Dictated by the spirit
ANDRE LUIZ

INTERNATIONAL SPIRITIST COUNCIL

ISBN 978-85-98161-28-0

B.N.
Original Title:
OS MENSAGEIROS
(Brazil, 1944)

Translators: Amy Duncan, Darrel W. Kimble and Marcia M. Saiz

1st Edition 2008 – published by the INTERNATIONAL SPIRITIST COUNCIL,
Brasília, (BR) – 1st impression 2.000

000.2-O; 3/2008

Cover design by: Claudio Carvalho and Luis Hu Rivas

Layout: Claudio Carvalho

Edition of
INTERNATIONAL SPIRITIST COUNCIL
Av. L-2 Norte – Q. 603 – Conjunto F (SGAN)
70830-030 – Brasília (DF) – Brazil

Authorized edition by Federação Espírita Brasileira

Printed and bound by
the Editorial and Graphics Department of Federação Espírita Brasileira
Rio de Janeiro (RJ) – Brazil
CNPJ nº 33.644.857/0002-84 *I.E. nº 81.600.503*

CIP-BRASIL. CATALOGAÇÃO-NA-FONTE
SINDICATO NACIONAL DOS EDITORES DE LIVROS, RJ.

L979m

Luiz, Andre (Spirit)
The messengers: (a mediumistic work) / [received by] Francisco Cândido Xavier; dictated by the Spirit Andre Luiz; [translated by Amy Duncan, Darrel W. Kimble and Marcia M. Saiz]. – Brasília, DF (Brazil): International Spiritist Council, 2008

336p.: 21cm

Translated from: Os Mensageiros

ISBN 978-85-98161-28-0

1. Spiritualism. 2. Spirit writings. I. Xavier, Francisco Cândido, 1910-2002. II. Conselho Espírita Internacional. III. Title.

08-0814. CDD 133.93
CDU 133.7

03.03.08 04.03.08 005568

CONTENTS

The messengers 9

1 – Renewal 13

2 – Aniceto 19

3 – At the Messenger Center 25

4 – Vicente's story 31

5 – Listening to Instructions 37

6 – Profound Warnings 45

7 – Otavio's Downfall 51

8 – Acelino's Downfall 59

9 – Listening to Impressions 65

10 – Joel's Experience 71

11 – Belarmino the Instructor 77

12 – Monteiro's Account 83

13 – Vicente's Reflections 89

14 – Preparations 95

15 – The Journey 101

16 – At the Rescue Outpost 107

17 – Alfredo's Love Story 113
18 – Information and Explanations 119
19 – Breath 127
20 – Defenses against Evil 133
21 – Demented Spirits 141
22 – Those who Sleep 149
23 – Nightmares 155
24 – Ismalia's Prayer 161
25 – Her Prayer's Effects 167
26 – Listening to the Workers 173
27 – The Slanderer 179
28 – Social Life 187
29 – Interesting News 195
30 – In friendly Conversation 201
31 – Cecilia at the Organ 207
32 – A Sublime Melody 213
33 – En Route to Earth 219
34 – Nosso Lar's Support Post 225
35 – Home Worship 231
36 – Mother and Children 237
37 – In the Home Sanctuary 243
38 – Hard at Work 249
39 – Never-ending Work 255
40 – Heading to the Countryside 261
41 – Among the Trees 267
42 – The Word in a Rural Setting 273
43 – Before the Meeting 279

44 – Assistance 285
45 – The Infirm Mind 291
46 – Continuing to Learn 297
47 – Hard at Work – Again 303
48 – The Dread of Death 309
49 – The Divine Machine 315
50 – Fernando's Discarnation 321
51 – Saying Goodbye 329

The Messengers

This book describes some of the experiences of spirit messengers. Because the landscapes, observations, acts and events it depicts seem so physical, many readers will undoubtedly conclude – according to old philosophical concepts – that "it's all a product of the human brain."

One must realize, however, that the brain is the apparatus of reasoning, and that by way of the simple event of physical death, discarnate humans do not suddenly enter the realms of the angels. On the contrary, they continue to face their own conscience, struggling to enlighten their minds, and in a different vibratory sphere they prepare to continue their journey toward perfection.

No one can negate the laws of evolution.

If a chimpanzee were to rise to the status of living in a palace and found a way to write to others at the same stage of evolution, it would find almost no fundamental differences to describe, because of the similarities between it and its fellow creatures. It would tell other chimps about a more improved animal life, and perhaps the only aspect impossible for it to define would be the aureole of reason surrounding the human spirit. As for ways of life per se, the change would not be profoundly perceptible. Simple animal fur would find continuity in modern cashmeres and silks. The order of nature surrounding the jungle nest would be the same that provides stability to the human home. The cave will have been transformed into a stone building. The green meadow would be likened to the cultivated garden. The means of continuing the species would present nearly identical phenomena. The law of heredity would continue with minor modifications. The same tendencies would be displayed regarding nutrition. The unity of family kinship would reveal the same strong ties. Thus, the chimpanzee would only find it difficult to try to detail the problems of work, responsibility, an enriched memory, a purified sentiment and spiritual growth; in short, all the problems related to the acquisition of reason.

In light of that, there is no real justification for the amazement of those who read messages of the caliber of the ones that Andre Luiz addresses to individuals who are devoted to their spiritual growth.

Ordinary men and women are used to eagerly hoping for something extraordinary to happen. They forget that nature is not concerned with satisfying their individual, particular point of view.

Physical death is not an unbalanced leap; it is merely one evolutionary step.

Like our chimp, who discovered an ennobled animal life in the human environment, the human who, after his or her physical death, merits entry into the exalted circles of the Invisible, discovers an uplifted human life.

Naturally, a great number of higher-level spiritual problems await individuals there, challenging their understanding as they ascend sublimely toward the illumined realms of life. Progress does not grind to a halt at death; souls move on incessantly, attracted by the Light of Immortality.

However, the philosophical conclusions of this simple preface are not what have induced us to write it, but rather the need to disclose to our friend, the reader, holy opportunities for work during these trying times.

Happy are they who seek in the New Revelation[1] *their place of service while on earth – their place in harmony with the will of God.*

Christian Spiritism does not offer humankind only an area of research and consultation to be tread honorably by the rare, studious individual; it does much more than that: it reveals a workshop of renewal where each consciousness-in-training must seek his or her rightful integration into the higher life through inner effort, self-discipline and self-improvement.

There is no lack of divine cooperation for the willing worker. And whoever observes the noble work of an Aniceto will realize that it is not easy for spirits to offer assistance to humans. Bringing the fraternal collaboration of the higher

[1] That is, Spiritism. – Tr.

planes down to incarnate spirits is not some mechanical process based on principles of least effort. So that they may receive such aid, human beings cannot escape the imperative to wash the vessel of their hearts in order to receive the "living water," to take off their worldly rags in order to put on the "wedding garments" of eternal light.

Thus, happy at having finished our duty, dear reader, we present you with these new pages by Andre Luiz. They consist of a partial report of one week of spirit work by messengers of the good as they work alongside incarnate humans. Above all, they portray the character of a conscientious emissary and generous benefactor in the person of Aniceto, and they stress the need for moral discipline for those who consecrate themselves to the noble activities of the faith in the arena of service.

My friend, if you are seeking the spiritual light, if animal-like existence has wearied your heart, remember that in spiritualism, investigation always leads to the infinite in the realm of the infinitesimal as well as in the sphere of the distant stars, and only the transformation of yourself in the light of Higher Spirituality will enable you to draw from the founts of the Divine Life. And above all, remember that these uplifting messages from the beyond are not meant to be a mere expression of emotion; above all, they are intended for your understanding as a child of God so that you will take inventory of your own accomplishments and truly hand yourself over to the responsibility of living in the presence of the Lord.

EMMANUEL

Pedro Leopoldo, Brazil, February 26, 1944

1

Renewal

Having disengaged myself from the lower ties that had bound me to earthly concerns, I felt a higher understanding now gladdening my spirit.

Such liberation had not happened all at once, however.

Deep down, I realized how difficult it had been for me to leave behind the surroundings of my home, and how hard it had been to bear my wife's lack of understanding and my beloved children's differences of opinion.[1]

I felt certain that selfless and powerful spirit friends had helped my poor and imperfect soul make such an important transition.

---

[1] See *Nosso Lar*, Ch. 49. – Tr.

Previously, concern for my wife had tortured my heart incessantly, but now that I had come to accept the fact that she was deeply involved with her second husband, there was nothing left to do but to seek out other interests.

It was thus that, thoroughly amazed, I noticed my self-transformation as events unfolded.

I was living the joy of self-discovery. Until now, I had been living like a mollusk tucked away in its shell, oblivious to the lofty splendors of nature as it crawls around in the mud. However, I was convinced that my grief had tilled my mental processes like a heavy hoe, whose thrusts I had not understood right away. That hoe had broken through the shell of my former, corrupted sentiments and had set me free. My spirit body had been exposed to the sun of infinite goodness, and I had begun to see higher, reaching out to further distances.

For the first time, I regarded my adversaries as benefactors. I had begun to visit my earth family again no longer as master of the domestic circle, but as a worker who loves his job in the workshop to which life has assigned him. I no longer saw my wife as a companion who had failed to understand me, but as a sister whom I should help as much as my strength allowed. I refrained from regarding her second husband as an intruder who had changed my plans, but rather as a brother who needed the help that my own experiences could offer. I no longer considered my children as my property but as very dear companions, and it behooved me to extend to them the benefits of my new knowledge and to support them spiritually as much as I possibly could.

After having been compelled to destroy my castles of unwarranted exclusivity, I felt another kind of love settling into my soul.

I had been orphaned by earthly affections but had become receptive to the higher designs that had traced out a different course for my destiny. I had begun to hear the profound and divine call of universal consciousness.

Only now did I realize how far removed I had lived from the sublime laws that govern human evolution.

Nature was welcoming me with raptures of love, and its voices were now much stronger than those of my personal interests. Bit by bit, I had begun to reap the joy of listening to its mysterious teachings in the grand silence of things. The simplest elements had begun to take on extraordinary meaning. The spirit colony that had generously taken me in was displaying new expressions of indefinable beauty: the rustling of a bird's wings, the whisper of the wind and the light of the sun seemed to reach into my soul, filling my thoughts with wondrous harmony.

The spirit life, inexpressible and beautiful, had opened resp andlendent portals. Until now, I had lived in Nosso Lar[1] like a sickly guest in a shiny palace. I had been so entirely wrapped up in myself that I was incapable of perceiving its enchantment and marvels.

Spiritually uplifting conversation had become indispensable.

---

[1] A spirit colony and backdrop for events described in the book by the same name. – Tr.

I used to enjoy torturing my soul with memories of earth. I used to appreciate the dramatic stories of various fellow spirits in that struggle, remembering my own case and becoming infatuated with the prospect of clinging once again to my earth relatives and resorting to such inferior ties. But now ... I had completely lost my passion for less-than-worthy matters. Even the stories told by the patients in the Chambers of Rectification did not hold as much interest as before. I no longer desired to know where those unfortunate creatures had come from, and I no longer pried into the adventures they had experienced in the lower zones. Instead, I sought out brothers and sisters in need. I wanted to know how I could be useful to them.

Perceiving this profound transformation, Narcisa said to me one day:

"Andre, my friend, you have been undergoing mental renewal. During such times, extreme troubles of a spiritual nature assault our hearts. Remember to meditate on the Gospel of Jesus. I know that you have been experiencing inexpressible joy in your contact with universal harmony after having left your whimsical designs behind, but I also know that along with the roses of joy and the new paths that are opening up to your hopes, there have been thorns of weariness on the edges of the old inferior roads that you are leaving behind. Your heart is a chalice illuminated by the rays of the divine dawn, but it has been emptied of the worldly sentiments that filled it for many centuries."

I myself could not have formulated such an exact description of my spiritual state.

Narcisa was right. Supreme joy was indeed flooding my spirit, but it was coupled with an unfathomable sensation of weariness regarding matters of a lower nature. I felt free of a number of heavy shackles, but I no longer had a home, a wife or my beloved children. I frequently returned to my former home and worked there for the good of all, but I felt no real incentive. My devoted friend had been correct. My heart certainly was a luminous chalice – an empty one, though. Her definition had touched me.

Sensing my silent tears, Narcisa added:

"Fill your chalice with the eternal waters of the One who is the Divine Giver. All of us, Andre, are bearers of the Christ plant within the soil of our hearts. During periods such as the one you are going through, it is easier for us to develop successfully if we know how to take advantage of the opportunities. As long as humans' minds are engulfed merely in reasoning and making calculations, the Gospel of Jesus appears as nothing more than a collection of ordinary teachings to them; however, when their higher sentiments are awakened, they realize that the Master's lessons have a life of their own, that they reveal expressions unknown to their minds to the degree that they make the effort to edify themselves as instruments of the Father. When we grow in the Lord, his teachings also grow in our sight. Let us do good, my dear! Fill your chalice with the unction of divine love. Since you have already felt the rays of the new dawn, walk confidently into the day!"...

And knowing my human temperament, an enthusiast of hectic work, she added kindly:

"You have worked long enough here in the Chambers, where I have been preparing myself for my next life in the flesh. I will not be able to accompany you, but I believe you should take advantage of the new service courses at the Ministry of Communication.[1] Many of our coworkers have been trained to lend help to incarnates. They work both in the visible and invisible realms, and all of them are supervised by worthy instructors. You might enjoy new experiences, learn a great deal and make an excellent individual contribution. Why not give it a try?"

Before I could thank Narcisa for this valuable suggestion, she was called to service in the Chambers, leaving me overwhelmed by expectations that were different than I had previously had regarding my duties.

---

[1] One of the six Ministries into which *Nosso Lar* is divided. See *Nosso Lar*, ch. 8, p. 58. – Tr.

2

Aniceto

I told Tobias about my new plans and couldn't help noticing the look of satisfaction that spread across his face.

"Don't worry," he said kindly, "you have the necessary number of work hours to justify your request. We have a large number of colleagues in Communication, so it won't be hard to place you with amiable instructors. Have you met our esteemed Aniceto?"

"I haven't had the pleasure."

"He is a former coworker," he amiably continued to explain. "He was with us in Regeneration for some time. Afterwards, he devoted himself to self-sacrificing duties in the Ministry of Assistance, and today he is a qualified instructor at the Ministry of Communication, where he has been providing noteworthy assistance. I'll talk it over with Minister Genesio. Don't be concerned. We regard your desire as being very praiseworthy, Andre."

My esteemed friend left me in a sea of inexpressible contentment.

I had begun to understand the value of work. Narcisa and Tobias' friendship was an unspeakably generous treasure, which the spirit of service had revealed to my soul.

A new area of struggle was about to unfold to my soul. I could not miss this chance. Nosso Lar was full of spirits who were anxious for an opportunity like this. Wouldn't it be to my advantage to offer myself willingly to this new learning experience? Also, because I was sure that I would be returning to the flesh in the not too distant future, such an arrangement would represent an extremely important undertaking for my overall self-improvement.

A mysterious joy overwhelmed me completely, and a sublime hope illuminated my sentiments. Narcisa had aroused in me an ardent desire to work on behalf of others, and it now seemed to fill the empty vessel of my heart.

Yes, I would work. I would come to know the satisfaction of working anonymously for the happiness of others, and would seek the wondrous light of fraternity by serving them.

That night Tobias came looking for me. Always obliging, he brought me comforting news of Minister Genesio's acquiescence.

With a loving smile, he invited me to accompany him. He was going to take me to Aniceto so that we could discuss the matter.

I was filled with overwhelming excitement as I followed him to the home of the new personage who was about to be fundamentally linked to my life as a spirit from then on.

Unlike Tobias, Aniceto had not been spiritually married to anyone in Nosso Lar.[1] He was living with five of his former disciple friends from earth in a comfortable building nestled among leafy, peaceful trees that stood like sentries guarding the extensive and marvelous rose garden.

His kindly welcome made an excellent impression on me. He exuded the calm appearance of a man who had reached maturity without the delusions of inexperienced youth. Although his face expressed great enthusiasm, it revealed the healthy optimism of a heart filled with sacred ideals. He listened very serenely to my benefactor as he explained my situation, casting friendly and searching glances at me from time to time.

Tobias spoke at length. He mentioned that I had been a doctor on the earth plane, but that I was now readjusting my values on the spirit plane.

After observing me attentively, Aniceto offered:

"I don't see why anything would keep us from doing this, my dear Tobias, but we must realize that it

[1] See *Nosso Lar* Chapter 38, Tobias' Case. – Tr.

depends on the candidate. You are aware that this colony is known as the 'Institution of the New Human.'"

"Andre is ready and willing," my friend said affectionately.

Aniceto gave me a penetrating look and warned:

"The work we do is varied and demanding. The department under our responsibility only accepts workers interested in discovering the joy of serving others. We are mutually committed not to complain about anything at all. No one expects personal praise for having completed a useful task, and we all answer for any errors we might commit. We here are in the process of extinguishing the old personal vanities that we have brought from earth. Within the hierarchical mechanism of our obligations, we are interested only in the divine good. We realize that every constructive opportunity comes from our Father, and this conviction helps us ignore the improper demands of our lower self."

Noticing my surprise, Aniceto made a meaningful gesture and continued:

"For the emergency work, whose objective is to prepare active coworkers, we have a supplementary staff that has fifty openings for trainees. At the moment, I have three openings left. The instructive activity is intense for those who will be providing emergency aid down on earth. Some instructors are accompanied by all their trainees as they perform their services there, but I have adopted a different approach. I usually divide my class into specialized groups according to the professions the students are familiar with so that they can make the best use of their preparation and practice. I currently have a Roman Catholic priest, a doctor, six engineers, four teachers, four nurses, two painters, eleven women specializing in domestic work and eighteen laborers of various types. In Nosso Lar, we carry out the activities entrusted to us as a group, but on days when I work down on earth, not all of my students come with me. Of course, the engineers or laborers, for example, would not be denied the opportunity to acquire other knowledge that reaches beyond the realm of duties under their specialized responsibility, but it would have to consist of self-initiated efforts during the ample time that everyone receives for rest and entertainment. With regard to our current service, then, we are interested in making the best use of our time not only to benefit those who need our fraternal aid but also to help ourselves in terms of effectiveness."

I was amazed as I pondered this curious approach while Aniceto took a long pause.

After submersing all his attention in me as if he wanted to perceive the effect of his words, he continued:

"The purpose of this method is not just to create more obligations for others. Here, as on earth, the one who actually learns the most in classes and demonstrations is not the student but the instructor, who enriches his observations and deepens his level of experience. When Minister Espiridiao recruited me for this job, I accepted on condition that I would not waste any time on behalf of my own betterment and education. Therefore, I don't need to extend myself to other matters.

I think I've said enough for now. If you are willing, I can't possibly turn you down."

"I understand your most-noteworthy program," I responded emotionally. "It would be an honor to accompany you and receive your orders to serve."

The look on Aniceto's face indicated that I had given him the answer he was looking for, and so he concluded:

"Very well, you may begin tomorrow."

Turning to Tobias, he added:

"Early tomorrow morning, send our friend to the Messenger Center. We will be involved in active study there and will make sure that Andre is given the bonuses[1] according to Communication's guidelines."

Quite pleased, we thanked him. Then I said goodbye to Tobias, filled with a new sense of hope.

---

[1] A reference to the hour-bonus – the non-monetary standard of payment in *Nosso Lar*. See *Nosso Lar*, Ch. 22.

3

At the Messenger Center

The next day, I listened to Narcisa's lengthy, thoughtful comments on my new endeavor, and then headed for the Messenger Center in the Ministry of Communication. The always helpful Tobias went along in spite of the huge amount of work he still had to do.

I was fascinated when we arrived at the group of majestic buildings that comprised the institution's headquarters. The complex was so big that I could have sworn I had come upon what looked like several universities linked together. Wide patios filled with groves and gardens invited uplifting inner reflection.

Tobias aroused me from my enchantment and exclaimed:

"The Center is very large. This department of our spirit colony performs some very complex activities. Don't think that the buildings we can see from this spot are all there is to the institution. This part contains only the central administration and a few buildings for general teaching and preparation."

"But is this huge organization restricted only to transmitting messages?" I asked curiously.

My companion smiled meaningfully and explained:

"Don't get the idea that this is all just a type of postal service. The Center prepares spirits for the purpose of transforming them into 'living letters' of rescue and aid to other spirits who are suffering in the Umbral,[1] on earth's surface and in the Darkness. Could you really believe that so much work was just meant for broadcasting news? Broaden your outlook! Our service here is a copy of the type of service that is being carried out in the most diverse spirit cities of the higher planes. Many, many spirits are prepared here to spread hope and consolation, and to provide instruction and counsel in the various arenas of the planet's evolution. I don't mean just invisible emissaries, however. We also train tightly-knit groups for reincarnation, and mediums and instructors leave here by the hundreds every year. Those who will be involved in giving spiritual comfort are trained by our Messenger Center and are sent to the incarnate realms in considerable numbers."

---

[1] The Umbral is "...situated between heaven and earth, and is the doleful region of darkness built and cultivated by the human mind, which is in most cases rebellious, lazy, confused and feeble." (Xavier, Francisco Candido, *Ação e Reação* (Action and Reaction): Federação Espírita Brasileira (Brazilian Spiritist Federation), 1994 (Translation ours). – Tr.

"What are you saying?" I asked, surprised. "According to what you have stated then, their work of providing spiritual enlightenment should be extremely developed in the world!..."

Tobias gave me an odd look, smiled serenely and explained:

"My dear Andre, you haven't considered the fact that this preparation in and of itself doesn't mean they'll be successful. Thousands of qualified messengers leave, but the ones who actually succeed are quite rare indeed. Some manage to accomplish their task partially, but most others fail completely. Real service is not just an idea; it involves effort, without which the work can neither begin nor prevail. Ranks of mediums and instructors leave here for the physical world with special training, because benefactors of Higher Spirituality need selfless and altruistic mediums in order to enhance humankind's redemption. But when these messengers forget their missionary spirit and their dedication to their fellow beings, they usually become worthless instruments. There are mediums and mediumship, doctrinal instructors and doctrine, just as there are plows and farmers. A plow may be excellent, but if the farmer lacks the desire to use it, all the plow will inevitably produce is rust. The same applies to psychic faculties and great knowledge. Mediums may be endowed with a very powerful mediumistic ability, but if they cannot see beyond their own interests, they will completely fail in their assigned task. Believe me, my dear friend, all constructive work carries with it its corresponding struggle. Those who endure the hardships and setbacks of the front lines are very rare indeed. An overwhelming percentage of mediums avoid facing the heavy gunfire. Countless workers retreat just at the moment when the task offers the most valuable opportunity."

Quite impressive, I thought.

"That really surprises me. I never imagined that such messengers were prepared here for life in the physical realm."

"Ah! My friend," said Tobias, smiling, "did you really think that the work of doing good would be limited to simple automatic circumstances? On earth, our spiritual sight tends to get tarnished by outward expressions of worship and religious activity, leading us to believe we can resolve any problem with a prayer-like posture. However, getting down on one's knees doesn't resolve the fundamental questions of the spirit, nor does the greatest spiritual growth entail merely worshiping the Divine One. The truth is that every act of humility and love is worthy of respect and is holy, and the Lord undoubtedly will grant us his blessings; nonetheless, it is imperative to remember that maintaining and keeping the vessel clean enough to receive such blessings is a duty that is fitting for us. So, we do not prepare mere 'postal clerks' at this Center, but spirits who have become living letters from Jesus to incarnate humankind. At least that is the program as defined by our spirit administration..."

Moved, I fell silent, pondering the grandeur of these teachings. After a long pause, my companion proceeded:

"Because we are almost all still linked to a long history of heinous wrongdoings that have deformed our personalities, few of us succeed. In each new life of incarnate endeavor, we believe much more in the demeaning tendencies of our past than in the divine potential of the present, a fact which always has negative implications for the future. And so that is how we proceed there. We cling to evil and forget the good, sometimes foolishly interpreting our difficulties as forms of punishment, whereas for those of us who have 'eyes to see', every obstacle offers a truly precious opportunity for growth."

At this point we reached an enormous enclosure.

Hundreds of spirits were pouring into the large building, whose stairs we ascended in lively conversation.

The features of the marvelous atrium impressed me with their imposing beauty. Varieties of flowers, previously unknown to me, adorned the porticos, spreading lively colors and delectable fragrances.

Breaking my enchantment, Tobias explained:

"The various groups of trainees are heading for their classes. Let's look for Aniceto in the teachers' department.

We went down vast hallways, encountering veritable crowds of spirits involved in animated conversation while looking for their classrooms.

We found our obliging friend from the previous evening as part of a small group that seemed to be involved in a very discreet conversation. He embraced us serenely with a smile.

"Well, well!" he said, kindly and good-naturedly. "I've been expecting our new student since early this morning."

Tobias explained that he was in a great hurry, so the noble instructor explained:

"From now on, Andre will be under my care. Go back in peace."

I was filled with emotion as I said goodbye to my companion.

Noticing my natural timidity, Aniceto asked a service assistant:

"Call Vicente for me, would you?"

And turning back to me, he explained:

"Vicente has been my only medical trainee until now. I'll put you together because of your professional affinity."

Less than three minutes passed before Vicente was standing in front of us.

"Vicente," said Aniceto matter of factly, "this is Andre Luiz, our new coworker. He used to be a doctor like yourself. I believe you will feel at ease with each other because you share the same background."

Vicente embraced me, showing how pleased he was, and after encouraging me with beautiful, stimulating words, he asked our guide:

"When should we look for you for today's studies?"

Aniceto thought for a moment and replied:

"Explain our regulations to our new candidate and join us for instructions right after noon."

4

Vicente's story

I couldn't possibly express how happy I was with my newfound friendship.

Vicente had a very peaceful looking face; it displayed an expression of intelligence and lucidity, and radiated affection and goodness, sensibility and understanding.

He told me he was overjoyed at having found a fellow physician, and he arranged a room for me conveniently close to his, demonstrating his great fraternal kindness.

He was my first colleague from my former profession. He too had recently arrived from the spheres of earth, and he was the first with whom I felt a more direct connection.

We freely exchanged ideas about the surprises that we had encountered since our arrival. We commented on the problems resulting from worldly misconceptions, the myopia of the planet's limited medicinal science, and the profound and fascinating issues surrounding spirit medicine.

Although Vicente had not yet made any visits to the incarnate plane in a service capacity, he had an extraordinary admiration for Aniceto, and brought me up to date on the valuable studies they had delved into together.

He was full of enthusiastic ideas. In a little over an hour, our friendship had become like the sentiment of two brothers who had been united by spiritual ties for a long time. My new companion had won my boundless trust.

Displaying great tact, he asked about my situation regarding my earth relatives, and I responded with a brief account of my unusual adventure when I had learned of my widow's second marriage. I told my story as expressively as possible, becoming quite emotional during my narrative. With each culminating particular of what had occurred, I intentionally slowed down my account, emphasizing my former sufferings and relating seemingly insurmountable adversities.

Vicente listened in silence, smiling from time to time.

When I finished my moving account, he placed his right hand on my shoulder and murmured:

"You mustn't think you were unfortunate and misunderstood. You should realize, my dear Andre, that, in fact, you were extremely fortunate."

"What do you mean?"

"Your Zelia respected you as a companion to the last of your days, and under such circumstances a second marriage is not at all surprising. In my case, however, things were much worse."

Given my understandable surprise, my new friend continued:

"Let me explain."

He thought for a few seconds as if he were putting his memories in order, and then proceeded:

"You can't imagine how intense a dream of love my marriage was. Soon after receiving my professional diploma at age twenty-five, I married Rosalinda. I was radiant with happiness. I brought my wife not only into a comfortable and secure financial situation but also into the treasures of my affection and devotion. My happiness knew no bounds. In a short time, two little children enriched our happy home. My sense of well-being was inexpressible. Because of my bank reserves, I didn't have to specialize in clinical work, but instead devoted myself passionately to the laboratory. Because of my propensity for that type of work, it wasn't long before I gained the trust of many colleagues and various study centers, which resulted in increased research opportunities and shining results. Rosalinda was my primary and most capable coworker. From time to time, she got bored handling test tubes, but she was able to repress such little annoyances for the sake of our domestic happiness. She seemed to understand me completely. In my eyes, she was a dedicated mother and a flawless companion.

"Well, ten years of conjugal bliss had passed when my brother Eleuterio, an unmarried lawyer somewhat older than myself, decided to settle close by. Rosalinda went out of her way to be attentive to him since he was a member of my family. Eleuterio came into our home as a true brother. Although he actually roomed in a hotel, he took part in our evenings at home, and was always charming and eager to please.

From that time on, though, I noticed that my wife had begun changing little by little. She demanded that I hire an assistant to replace her at work, claiming that our little ones needed more dedicated, maternal attention. I happily consented. After all, it was an arrangement that was important for our children's welfare. However, Rosalinda's transformation started to become more noticeable. She began to avoid the laboratory altogether, where we had happily embraced so many times after seeing our most important experiments crowned with success. She preferred to go to the cinema or to a retreat with Eleuterio.

I was greatly saddened by this, but I had no reason to doubt my brother's behavior. He had always been considerate at home, although he was bold and egotistical in his professional life.

My home life, which had always been so happy, had now become one of rather bitter loneliness, which I tried to evade with persistent, honest work.

"Things continued like that, when an odd transformation altered my life. A small pustule in one of my nostrils had never bothered me in any way before, but after I injured it slightly, it turned into an extremely serious condition. In just a few hours, it broke out in septicemia. My colleagues gathered around my sickbed in a veritable assembly. However, all their care was useless; their best attempts at helping me were null and void and I realized that my end was rapidly approaching. Rosalinda and Eleuterio appeared to be heart-stricken and even now I can see their looks of anguish at the moment when the mist of death shrouded my corporeal eyes."

At this point, Vicente remained quiet for a long while as if focusing on his most painful memories, and then he continued, less enthusiastically:

"After a period of pitiful troubles in the lower zones, and after I had recovered in Nosso Lar, I discovered the whole truth. Upon returning to my earth home, I was in for a big surprise: Rosalinda was now married to Eleuterio."

"Our stories are almost identical!" I exclaimed.

"Not really," he protested with a smile.

And he continued:

"Another surprise rent my heart. Only when I returned to my home did I learn that I had been the victim of a hateful crime. My own brother had devised the deviously wicked plot. My wife and he had fallen hopelessly in love and had yielded to the temptations of the flesh. Divorce was not possible. Even if the law had allowed it, it would have been scandalous for Rosalinda to leave me to publicly live with her brother-in-law. However, Eleuterio remembered that she and I had worked in the laboratory together and he suggested that she infect me with a certain microbial culture, which he took upon himself to obtain as soon as possible. My poor wife wasted no time, and taking the opportunity while I was asleep, she injected the deadly virus into the tiny, slightly opened pustule.

"And that's my story in a nutshell."

I was dumbstruck.

"And those criminals?" I asked.

Vicente smiled slightly and said:

"Rosalinda and Eleuterio are apparently living together quite happily; they are dedicated materialists for the time being, and are enjoying their great fortune and high social standing in the transitory world."

"But... what about justice?" I inquired, disturbed.

"Look Andre," he calmly explained, "everything comes in its time – the good as well as the bad. First the seed; then, the fruit."

Noticing how sad I looked, however, Vicente concluded:

"Let's not talk about this any more. It's almost time for class. Let's attend to our essential needs and help our loved ones, who are still far away in the earthly circles. Don't be too concerned. In order to produce fruit, the tree doesn't complain about its dead leaves. For us at this time, my friend, evil is the mere result of ignorance and nothing more."

5

Listening to Instructions

Aniceto was waiting for us in the large, welcoming hall.

Long rows of assistants filled the huge area.

Men and women of apparently different ages seemed to be lost in thought, but nevertheless displayed expectation and interest.

"Today," explained our guide, addressing Vicente in particular, "we are going to hear a talk by Telesforo, a former worker at the Ministry of Communication. He has requested the presence of all trainees involved in the communication efforts between us and our incarnate brothers and sisters.

We in turn sat down and made ourselves comfortable.

A few minutes later, Telesforo entered the sanctuary to the harmonious vibrations of general congeniality.

Aniceto and other instructors took their places next to him around a stately table, where others in charge of the assembly were also seated.

After greeting the large audience, Telesforo offered us his wishes of peace, and encouraged us to give testimonies regarding our redemptive experiences. He then proceeded to the main subject that had brought him there.

"Now," he said authoritatively yet simply, "we will address the need for representation from our colony in work to be done down on earth. There are fellow spirits here who failed to complete their worthily conceived objectives, and other brothers and sisters who wish to take part in tasks that involve our current responsibilities. We are of course referring to Communication's painstaking activities on the physical plane. At this gathering, there are a large number of Nosso Lar's coworkers who failed in their missions of mediumship and instruction, as well as many others who are now preparing themselves for just such trials in the corporeal sphere.

"Our division has been involved in promoting a large operation designed to aid those of our incarnate and discarnate brothers and sisters who have proven to be incapable of functioning beyond the terrestrial plane.

"We are faced with an enormous task. We need to dissiminate new teachings for preparing those who inhabit our colony, while at the same time taking into consideration present and upcoming efforts and achievements.

"It is vital to help those who are courageously facing the planet's profound changes.

"The fundamental changes of life on earth have found most people completely distracted from eternal realities. The human mind is becoming increasingly accepting and open to contact with the invisible realms, within which it functions and moves. This is a type of evolutionary fatalism. We desire to – indeed we must – aid incarnate individuals; nevertheless, vast waves of misunderstanding are working against the scope of our fraternal cooperation. We are not speaking merely of actions resulting from ignorance and perversity, but also of those great many forces of spiritualism itself that are opposed to us, and certain Christian teachings that are fighting against us as though we were not actually in accord with the Divine Master. The Church of Rome regards our work as diabolical. The various denominations of the Lutheran and Reformed churches persecute our well-intentioned efforts. And there are many other highly educated spiritualist schools which denounce our influence because they think that humans can become perfect overnight, immediately redeemed by an instantaneous stroke of will and without any effort at progress.

"In the arena of our understanding of life, however, we cannot condemn these groups for their lack of understanding for now. Roman Catholicism has its important reasons; Protestantism deserves our respect; the spiritualist schools possess noteworthy teachings. Every religious expression is sacred and every uplifting act of spiritual education is holy per se. Thus, what we are actually faced with is a lack of understanding by good institutions, and this comprises a dolorous trial for all of us sincere workers, because, after all, we are not doing individualistic work, but are fostering a liberating movement of human consciousness on behalf of the world's religious ideas.

"Clergy and theologians of the organized centers of religion and philosophy have not yet perceived that, just like the human soul, the spirit of revelation is progressive. Religious concepts evolve along with the mind of the individual. Many churches do not as yet understand that we must not spread the belief that unfortunate individuals are doomed to eternal torment. Instead, we must proclaim the certainty of there being hellish people creating their own personal hells.

"Nonetheless, we cannot waste time criticizing the stubbornness of others. We have complex and widespread services of our own to attend to. And, as we were saying, with every passing day, earth's humankind gets closer to the invisible sphere of lower vibrations surrounding them on all sides. But we realize that an overwhelming percentage of earth's inhabitants have not prepared themselves for today's evolutionary events. Highly agonizing conflicts are occurring in the human arena. Science is progressing at such a dizzying rate on the planet, and yet, as the afflictions of the body are overcome, those of the soul are multiplied. The world's newspapers are full of wonderful stories about material progress. Wondrous secrets of nature are being discovered in the realms of the sea, the land and the air, but statistics on human crime are frightening. The murders of war reveal levels of wickedness far beyond those known in former times. Homicides, suicides, marital tragedies, emotional misery, strikes, subversive revolutionary impulses, the thirst for degrading experimentation, sexual unrest, unknown diseases and insanity are invading human homes. In no country is there enough spiritual preparation for physical comfort; nevertheless, such comfort tends to increase naturally. Human beings will exert an increasing control over the exterior landscape of their planetary home, but they do not know themselves. When the body is heeded, however, it will reveal the needs of the soul, and we are now witnessing individuals being overwhelmed with serious problems not only due to their own deficiencies but also due to their close psychic proximity to the vibratory sphere of the millions of discarnates who cling to the planet's surface, anxious to renew the existence they formerly held in disdain and without the slightest concern for the designs of the Eternal One.

"Strictly speaking, we also understand that Communication's earth-related work should be carried out only on the level of divine inspiration toward the earthly realms, from the higher to the lower levels; however, how are we to reach the millions of sick individuals and criminals in the visible and invisible zones of human experience? Through mere ritualistic, outward worship, as the Church of Rome proposes? Through faith alone, as the Reformation churches claim? Through a mere affirmation of the will, as certain spiritualist schools expect? We cannot limit our opinions to a unilateral view of the problem, however. We agree that reverence toward the Father, faith and will are basic expressions of divine realization within the human being, but we cannot forget that labor is the fundamental need of every spirit. Let our other brothers and sisters continue with their theological speculations; let us, however, view the undertaking of the Lord's work as an indispensable duty.

"Humankind at this time is like a large collective organism, whose cells – i.e., individual humans – are involved in mutual instability in a worldwide process of readjustment and redemption.

"Those who work with us have seen the extent of the complications with which the human mind struggles. Criminals cling to other criminals; the sick associate with the sick. We need to offer the world instruments which are adequate for correcting the spirit, and which bestow upon our incarnate brothers and sisters a greater understanding of the spirit of Christ. To do this, however, we need faithful coworkers, who pay no mind to conditions, compensation or arguments, but who are interested in the sublimity of sacrifice and self-denial for the Lord."

At this point, Telesforo paused, and directing a penetrating glance at the gathering, said in a louder voice:

"Let those who do not wish to serve look for other kinds of work to do. The Ministry of Communication cannot allow wasting time on feeble experimentation, without doing serious harm to unwary coworkers. In the other Ministries, the assignment of workers characterizes with great precision all those who collaborate with the Divine Master. Here, however, more than just workers, we need servers who have a willing desire to assist."

At that moment, he took another long pause, during which I noticed how strong an impression he had made on the audience members, who were looking at each other with inexpressible amazement.

6

Profound Warnings

"Brothers and sisters," continued Telesforo, under the fervor of sacred inspiration, "we can hear the heartrending cries of earth's suffering souls. We need workers who wish to join the evangelical school of selflessness.

"Ever since Spiritism first began its task of renewing the world, Nosso Lar has sent various groups to work on spreading Spiritism's educative principles. Hundreds of fellow spirits leave here every year, combining their own need of redemption with redemptive service; however, we still have not achieved the results we desire. A few workers have enjoyed partial results in the tasks assigned to them, but most have failed miserably.

Our rescue institutions have set vital relief measures in motion, but to no avail. Very, very few have achieved any success as far as the intricate duties of mediumship and instruction are concerned.

"Other colonies on our plane are involved in providing services of the same nature; however, once on the 'other side of the veil', very few incarnates remember the eternal realities – ignorance dominates the minds of the majority. And ignorance is the mother of all misery, weakness and crime. When clothed in the fluids of the flesh, great instructors become frightened when confronted with human dissensions, and they seek unwarranted refuge in their own beliefs. They forget that Jesus did not expect human beings to attain his level of magnificent glory; instead, he came down to the human plane in order to love, teach and serve. He did not demand humans to become immediately like him; rather, he made himself to be like them in order to help them in their herculean ascent."

After a short pause and with a profound gleam in his eye, Telesforo stressed:

"If the Divine Master adopted this rule, what are we to say about our own obligations as failed individuals?

"Let us distance ourselves from the immense needs of other groups and identify what may be lacking in those who are closest to us.

"Personal ties around us constitute a broad field of activity for bearing witness.

"Let us abandon the idea that earth is a valley of darkness in which we are unfortunately doomed to fail, and let us take refuge in the certainty that the physical realm is a great redemptive workshop. Let us prepare ourselves to work effectively together. Let us forget the mistakes of the past and remind ourselves of our fundamental obligations.

"The general cause of failure in mediumistic work is the lack of a sense of responsibility and remembrance of the duty to be fulfilled.

"How many of you here were assisted by generous benefactors who sought to help you, commiserative of your cruel past? How many of you left here enthusiastically after having made prodigious promises? However, you were not able to repeat the task honorably in order to learn to serve according to the higher designs of the Eternal. Whenever the Lord provided for your physical needs, you yielded to unbridled ambition; faced with the merciful increase of intensified labor, you chose to cling to the idea of the easy life; instead of meaningful committed relationships, you preferred sexual forays; within your family circle, you turned to domestic tyranny, and upon the interests of the eternal life, you superimposed the ignoble suggestions of laziness and vanity. Most of you indulged in irresponsible conversation and undiscerning opinions, and became involved in countless useless activities. As mediums, many of you preferred remaining unaware of your faculty; as instructors, you formulated concepts for others, but never put them to your own use.

"What results have we achieved? Great masses flock to the wellsprings of sacred Spiritism only for the purpose of tainting its waters. Those who try to force open its doors are not seekers of the Kingdom of God, but rather seekers of their own personal interests. They crave a life of ease involving the least amount of effort; they are the lazy and delinquent ones in every situation, wanting to listen to discarnate spirits, but fearful of the accusations that their own conscience directs at them. The bile of doubt invades the balm of faith in well-intentioned minds. The longing for undeserved protection flagellates the followers of idleness. Ignorance and wickedness indulge in the evil manifestations of black magic.

"And why is all that, my brothers and sisters? Because we have not known how to defend the sacred trust; in our physical endeavors, we have forgotten that Spiritism is a divine revelation aimed at the fundamental renewal of human beings. We haven't yet considered how crucial it is to build the Kingdom of God within us.

"However, let us not abandon our duties in the middle of the task. Let us go back into the field to correct what we have sown. The Ministry of Communication has been stimulating this movement of renewal. We need willing workers who are loyal to the spirit of faith. Those who do not wish to learn of the glory hidden in the cross of witness will not be accepted, nor will those who have come here with different goals...

"Here we all are, fellow spirits in the Ministry of Communication, indebted to the world, but hopeful of success in our ongoing task. Let us look to heaven. Each and every day, the Lord gives us blessed new opportunities for work, but to attain the results we need, it is vital for us to forsake matters of a lower nature. Not one of us here is free from the cycle of reincarnation.

Therefore, we all yearn for the Eternal Life. So, let us not forget our Lord's Calvary; let us be convinced that every departure from the lower planes must lead to an ascent to the higher realms. And no one should expect to ascend spiritually without effort, sweat and tears!..."

At that moment, Telesforo ended his lecture, blessed the gathering, and with an infinitely radiant look, he accepted Aniceto's arm to lead him away.

As a result of the profound impression due to our instructor's incisive statements, I noticed that numerous onlookers were weeping silently.

At my questioning glance, Vicente explained:

"Those are workers who failed."

At that instant, Telesforo and Aniceto joined us.

Two ladies with serious looks on their faces approached respectfully, and one of them addressed Aniceto:

"We were wondering if you could kindly give us some information when Otavio will be granted his next opportunity to serve."

"The Ministry will let you know," answered Aniceto politely.

"But," repeated the questioner, "I would dare reiterate my request. It's that our good friend Marina, who got married on earth a few months ago, promised me that she would help him, and it would please me very much if I could find my poor son in new maternal arms."

Aniceto gave a gesture of understanding, smiled and explained simply:

"It is better not to carry out that plan for now. Before anything else, we need to come up with an answer for his failure as a medium. Only then, my sister."

I glanced back at Vicente without hiding my surprise, but as the ladies withdrew acceptingly, Aniceto said to us:

"I have some immediate matters to attend to with Telesforo. I shall leave everybody to their studies and observations here in the Messenger Center."

Aniceto left with the elders, and a fellow spirit said happily:

"We can talk now."

"Our guide," Vicente solicitously explained to me, "considers all healthy conversation to be useful work that enriches our learning and aptitudes for service. Thus, when we engage in spiritually constructive conversation, we receive the remuneration due for regular work."

Curious and surprised, I asked:

"And if I were to try going back to discussing earth-related topics and forget about spiritually constructive conversation?"

Vicente smiled and replied:

"That would be your loss, because here words define the spirit. If you were to avoid the light of instructive conversation, our guides would immediately recognize your attitude because your presence would become unpleasant and your face would be covered by indefinable darkness."

7

Otavio's Downfall

Aniceto's absence provided an opportunity for some interesting discussion.

We formed groups of friendly conversation.

I was impressed by the ladies who had asked for arrangements to be made for Otavio, so I asked Vicente to introduce me to them, not because I was moved by ordinary curiosity, but because I wanted to obtain new instructive insight into mediumistic work, which Telesforo's lecture had made me look at in a different light.

My friend kindly indulged me.

In a few moments, I found myself not only in the company of the sisters Isaura and Isabel, but of Otavio himself, a pale gentleman who looked to be about forty.

"I also am new here," I explained, "and my situation is that of a doctor who failed in the duties that the Lord entrusted to me."

Otavio smiled and replied:

"Perhaps, my friend, it worked to your advantage for having ignored the eternal truths when you were in the world. This is not true in my case, I'm sorry to say! I wasn't ignorant of the correct path that the Father had assigned to me for my struggles on earth. I possessed no official titles of competence; however, I received a noteworthy evangelical education, something that is of great importance for the eternal life and of greater importance than intellectual education per se. I had generous friends from the higher planes, and they made themselves visible to me; I received messages full of love and wisdom, yet I fell nonetheless, a slave to imprudence and vanity.

Otavio's remarks had a profound impact on me. When I was in the world, I had had no special contact with Spiritism and was experiencing a certain difficulty in understanding everything he wanted to say.

"I was unaware of the extent of the responsibilities involved in being a medium," I said.

"Spiritual duties," replied Otavio, somewhat downcast, "are concerned with eternal interests and that's why my failure was so enormous. The stewards of the soul's assets are endowed with extremely heavy responsibilities. The studious, the believers, the sympathizers in the arena of faith may allege ignorance and inhibition; however, the clergy have no excuse. The same applies to mediums. Disciples or beneficiaries in the 'temples' of the New Revelation may claim certain impediments, but the missionary must walk with a storehouse of such conviction that nothing can exonerate him from the guilt he amasses."

"But my friend," I asked, highly impressed, "what could have caused your moral immolation? You seem so aware of yourself, so highly informed about the laws of life, that it's hard to believe that you think you need new experiences in this chapter..."

Both of the ladies present had a strange sparkle in their eyes as Otavio replied:

"I will tell you about my downfall. You will see how I wasted a wonderful opportunity to evolve."

And after a longer pause, he continued grimly:

"After acquiring enormous debts in the physical realm in another lifetime, I came to knock at the gates of Nosso Lar, and was assisted by dedicated brothers and sisters, who worked tirelessly with me. Thus, for the next thirty years I prepared myself to return to earth to work as a medium, wishing to settle my accounts and to evolve in some way. There was no lack of truly sublime lessons or holy incentives for my imperfect heart. The Ministry of Communication did all they possibly could on my behalf, and six spirit friends in particular set great resources in motion to help me be successful. Technicians from the Ministry of Assistance accompanied me to earth on the day before my rebirth. I received a rigorously healthy physical body. According to the magnanimity of my benefactors here, I was to be granted greatly important work in the area of consoling other human beings. I would be among the ranks of workers in charge of Brazil, encouraging their efforts and assisting ignorant, disturbed or unhappy brothers and sisters. I wasn't to concern myself with marriage, not because it might interfere with my mediumship, but because my own particular case demanded that I not marry. Even though I was to be single, at the age of twenty I would welcome the six friends who had worked so hard for me in Nosso Lar, and who would arrive in my life as orphans. I had become greatly indebted to these spirits, and this provision would not only be a pleasant means of redemption for me, but also a guarantee of victory through my work of assisting them. This in turn would guard my heart against imprudence and distraction, because such a demanding livelihood would prevent me from succumbing to degrading ideas regarding sex and unrestrained ambition. It was also decided that my new activities would begin with much sacrifice so that any prospective affection from a possible wife wouldn't weaken my energy for achievement, so that my task wouldn't be enslaved to capricious worldly situations that were far outside Jesus' designs, and, above all, so that the impersonal nature of my service would be maintained. Thus, later on, over the years of my spiritual growth, I would be sent more and more material relief from Nosso Lar to the degree that I demonstrated self-denial, detachment from ephemeral possessions and disinterest in gratifying the senses, which would in turn enable me to progressively intensify the sowing of love entrusted into my hands.

"With everything in place, I went back, not only promising loyalty to my instructors, but also pledging the assurance of my devotion to my six spirit friends, to whom I owe so much, even now."

At this point, Otavio paused longer, sighed deeply, and continued:

"But alas, I forgot about every single one of my commitments! My benefactors in Nosso Lar placed me alongside a true servant of Jesus. My mother had been a Christian Spiritist since her youth, despite the materialistic tendencies of my father, who was, nevertheless, a moral man. At age thirteen my mother discarnated, and at fifteen I received the first calls from the higher realms. At that time, my father remarried, and in spite of the kindness and cooperation my stepmother offered me, I put myself on a plane of false superiority with regard to her. My birth mother directed sacred appeals to my heart from the invisible world, but to no avail. I was very rebellious, complaining unbecomingly. My relatives took me to a Spiritist group that had an excellent evangelical orientation, and where my faculties could be put to use for the needy and suffering; however, I lacked the character of a loyal and faithful worker. My refusal to trust in my spirit guides and my pronounced propensity for criticizing what others did drove me to an unpleasant standstill. My esteemed friends from the invisible realms encouraged me to serve, but in my unwholesome vanity I doubted them. And because the sacred calls continued – which I interpreted as hallucinations – I sought out a doctor, who told me that what I needed was sex. I had reached the age of nineteen and I yielded to the unbridled abuse of my sublime faculties. I wanted to force the harmony between sinful pleasure and spiritual duty, and this alienated me more and more from the evangelical teachings that friends from the higher spheres were ministering to us. I was little more than twenty years old when my father was snatched away by death. With this sad occurrence, six unfortunate children were orphaned, because when my stepmother married my father, she brought three little ones under his guardianship. In vain, the poor widow begged for my help. I never even pretended to accept the redemptive duties for which I was destined. After two years of her second widowhood, my unfortunate stepmother was taken to a leper colony. Filled with terror, I distanced myself from the little orphans. I abandoned them forever, without reflecting on the fact that I was delivering my generous creditors from Nosso Lar to an uncertain fate. Next, giving free reign to my indolence, I committed a dishonorable act and was forced to marry. Even then, however, the calls from the invisible world persisted, revealing the inexhaustible mercy of the Most High. But as I forgot my duties more and more, every attempt at spiritual accomplishment became more difficult. And so the tragedy that I had invented for my own torment continued. My wife, to whom I had gotten married only for unspeakably lustful purposes, was a creature much beneath my spiritual level. She was bonded to a monstrous spirit and attracted it to play the role of my son. The company of those six affectionate children would have contributed significantly to my moral security, but I had relegated them to the street; my spouse and son were in charge of exacting their revenge – so it seemed to me.

They both tormented me to the end of my days, whereupon I returned here barely having reached the age of forty, consumed by syphilis, alcohol and material woes ... having done nothing for my eternal future ... having constructed nothing in the arena of the good..."

He wiped his moist eyes and concluded:

"As you can see, I fulfilled all my damnable desires, but not the will of God. That is why I failed and exacerbated my old debts..."

At that instant, he fell silent as though something invisible had closed his throat.

I embraced him with brotherly sympathy, eager to offer his heart encouragement, but Dona Isaura[1] caressed his forehead and said:

"Don't cry, my son! Jesus doesn't withhold from us the blessing of time. Be calm and courageous..."

And recognizing her affection for him, I meditated on the Divine Goodness, whose sublime hymn is echoed in motherly love, even in the regions beyond the grave.

[1] In Brazilian society, *Dona* is a term of respect that is used with the woman's first name. – Tr.

8

Acelino's Downfall

I was going to speak some more with Otavio, but someone approached and said to the ex-medium in a firm voice:

"Don't cry, dear fellow. You haven't been forsaken. Besides, you can count on your mother's devotion. I'm in a worse situation, but even then I'm not without hope. We are obviously spiritually impoverished; however, we must wait confidently for a new loan of opportunity from the Divine Treasury. God is not poor."

I was surprised and turned around, but did not recognize the newcomer.

Dona Isaura politely introduced us.

It was Acelino, who had shared the same sort of experience as Otavio.

Noticing his sadness, Otavio smiled and warned:

“I’m not a criminal in the world’s eyes, but I’m a failure in God’s and Nosso Lar’s.

“Let’s be reasonable, though.” replied Acelino, seeming more upbeat. “You lost the match because you didn’t even play, whereas I lost it by playing disastrously. I went through eleven years of torment in the lower zones. Your situation didn’t demand such drastic measures. Even so, I trust in Providence.”

Just then, Vicente interrupted:

“Each one of us has had to experience what was appropriate for him. Not everyone succeeds in their trials on earth.”

And turning to me specifically, he explained:

“As doctors, how many of us have failed regretfully in the struggle?”

After agreeing and noting my own case, I countered:

“Nevertheless, it would be very interesting to hear about Acelino’s experience. Did he suffer the same misfortune as Otavio? I believe that delving into these lessons is very worthwhile. While incarnate, I didn’t have a good grasp on spiritual duty, but here our perspective changes. We have to think about our eternal future.”

Acelino smiled and replied:

"My story is quite different. My downfall displays different characteristics, and from my point of view, much more serious."

And meeting our expectations, he began his story:

"I too left Nosso Lar during the last century after receiving the valuable instructive heritage of our advisors. I went on my way, enriched with blessings. One of our distinguished Ministers in Communication presided personally over the measures related to my new task. There was no lack of resources to enable me to enjoy both bodily health and mental stability. After making a number of promises to our seniors, I left to serve our colony in one of the large cities of Brazil. Marriage was on my itinerary, and Ruth, my devoted companion, took it upon herself to work with me to better accomplish our tasks.

After finishing the first part of the plan at age twenty, I was called to mediumistic work and received tremendous support from invisible benefactors. I still remember the sincere satisfaction of my colleagues in the doctrinal group. The clairvoyant, clairaudient and psychographic faculties that the Lord had granted me out of his mercy were decisive factors for success in our work. Everyone was filled with unsurpassable joy. However, in spite of wonderful lessons regarding evangelical love, I was inclined to turn my faculties into a source of material income. I wasn't willing to wait for the abundant financial resources that the Lord was going to send me later on after I had proven myself, and I looked to solve my financial problems by myself. Wasn't my work the same as others'? Weren't Catholic priests paid for their spiritual and religious work? If we all had to pay for the needs of the body, why shouldn't we be paid for providing for the needs of the soul? My friends were ignorant of the sacred nature of faith, and so they approved of my selfish conclusions. We believed that discarnates were behind the essence of our work, but my personal collaboration as an intermediary was nonetheless part of it, for which payment would be appropriate.

My spirit friends rushed to point out a better way, but to no avail. In vain, my incarnate friends called for an appropriate explanation. I clung to my inferior interests and stuck to my own point of view, however. I would work only for paying clients. I determined what I would charge for consultations, with special rates for the poor and misfortunate. My consultation room filled up with people. Great interest was aroused among those desiring to improve their health and find solutions to their material affairs. A large number of wealthy families took me on as their regular consultant for all their life problems. Lessons regarding higher spirituality, friendly fellowship, redemptive work for the gospel and teachings by divine emissaries were left along the wayside. The school of virtue, fraternal love and higher edification no longer counted. Instead, business competition, legal or criminal relationships, passionate whims, police cases and a grand procession of humankind's miseries in their least worthy expressions were what mattered. The landscape of the spirit world encircling me had been completely transformed. By surrounding myself with criminals for monetary gain, the inferior mental currents of my troubled clients had incarcerated me in a dark psychic dungeon. I even committed the crime of ridiculing the

Gospel of our Lord Jesus, overlooking the fact that illicit business dealings with those who have corrupt scruples also entail involvement with evil spirits, who, on the invisible planes, show an interest in such dealings. I had transformed mediumship into a source of material hunches and cheap advice."

Just then our storyteller's eyes suddenly turned red, revealing unfathomable horror in their pupils as if he were reliving an atrocious torment.

"But death came, my friends, and tore me from my delusion," he continued more gravely. "At the moment of that great transition, the dark troupe of criminal clients who had preceded me to the grave surrounded me, demanding suggestions and guidance of a lower nature. They wanted news about incarnate accomplices and business results, and they demanded solutions regarding clandestine connections.

"I screamed, wept, implored, but I was shackled to them by sinister mental chains because of my imprudence in defending my spiritual heritage. For eleven years, I expiated my wrongdoings among them amidst remorse and bitterness."

Acelino fell silent and seemed even more distraught because of his abundant tears. Deeply touched, Vicente said:

"What's this? Don't beat yourself up like that. You didn't commit any murders, nor did you nourish any deliberate intentions to spread evil. The way I see it, you too deceived yourself like so many of us."

Acelino, however, dried his tears and replied:

"I wasn't a murderer or a common thief; I had no inner desire to hurt anyone, nor did I disrespect the homes of others. But I went to the physical realm to serve God's creatures – our brothers and sisters – alongside Jesus in order to help them in their spiritual growth. But I only made addicts of religious belief, and occult delinquents who were mutilated in their faith and crippled in their thought. I have no excuse, because I knew better; I can't be forgiven, for I didn't lack divine assistance."

And after a long pause, he concluded gravely:

"Now can you understand the extent of my guilt?"

9

Listening to Impressions

Allowing Acelino to converse in private with Otavio, Vicente led me to another part of the room.

Several groups were engaged in interesting and instructive conversation, and I noticed that nearly everyone was talking about the defeats they had suffered on earth.

"I did as much as I could!" exclaimed a kindly elderly lady to two of her friends, who were listening attentively. "Nonetheless, family ties were very strong. I continued to hear something within my spirit, a loud voice trying to make itself heard, compelling me to perform my task, but... what about my husband? Amancio had never accepted it. If unwell persons came to me in need of an ordinary *receituario*[1], his ill humor would worsen; if friends in the faith invited me to a Spiritist study session, he would carry on in a fit of jealousy. Would you believe he even went so far as to turn my own daughters against me? How could I have possibly attended to my mediumistic obligations under such circumstances?"

"Nevertheless," stated one of the women who seemed more self-assured, "we always find the means and pretexts to turn our backs on guilt. Let's take a realistic look at our problems. You must agree that with the help of a strong will you can always find a few minutes during the week and a few small opportunities to do good. Perhaps you could have won the understanding of your husband and the affectionate cooperation of your daughters if you had worked in silence, thereby demonstrating your sincere willingness to make a sacrifice. Our acts, Mariana, are much more contagious than our words."

"Yes," answered Mariana in a different tone of voice, "I agree with what you are saying. The truth of the matter is that I was never able to bear my family's lack of understanding without complaining about it."

"For us to work effectively," replied her friend judiciously, "we must know how to keep quiet above all else. We would have fulfilled our duties perfectly if we

---

1 The "Receituario" is the practice in some Brazilian Spiritist Centers of prescribing psychographed homeopathic or herbal medicines through special mediums called "receitistas." People come in, write the name and address of the person or themselves, and the requests are then passed on to these mediums, who then psychograph (at the command of the good spirits in charge) the appropriate medicine for each individual. – Tr.

ourselves had used all the guidelines for obedience and optimism that we offered to others. To give advice is always useful, but to give too much of it can make us forget our obligations. I say this bccausc my casc, I must admit, is very similar to yours. We went to the physical realm to grow with Jesus, but we fell into the foolishness of believing that we were on the earth to argue over our whims. I didn't perform my duty as a medium, because of my overpowering annoyance with respect to my family's indifference toward spiritual work. Our instructors here had previously advised me that in order to teach well it is necessary to set a good example. Unfortunately for me, however, I forgot all about that during my temporary work on earth. If my husband presented arguments against my spiritual work, I refuted them. I couldn't stand any opinion contrary to my own point of view in matters of faith, and I was incapable of perceiving the vanity and foolishness of my attitudes. Because of my thoughtlessness, I suffered my final loss, during which I greatly exacerbated my responsibilities. Joaquim and I fought almost every month and we exchanged not only hurtful insults but also poisonous fluids, secreted by our rebellious and sickly minds. Amidst these conflicts and their consequences, I wasted my time, unable to do any spiritually constructive work at all.

Just then, Vicente called me to introduce me to a friend.

Next to us, another group of women was engaged in lively conversation:

"So, Ernestina," one of them asked the youngest one, "what was the cause of your misfortune?"

"Simply put: fear, my friend," explained Ernestina. "I was afraid of everything and everyone. It was my greatest fault."

"Now that's surprising! You were very well prepared. I still remember our lessons together. The instructors from Elucidation placed significant trust in your competence. Your learning abilities set the standard for the rest of us."

"Yes, my dear Benita, but your memories make me feel more pointedly the extent of my personal spiritual impoverishment. However, I can't hide from the truth. I was to blame for everything. I had prepared myself well enough to pay off old debts and engage in new learning, but I was not as careful as I should have been. The call to service chimed at the right time and guided my thought processes to greater enlightenment; our instructors offered me the holiest incentives, but I distrusted other people, discarnates and even myself. In my instructors on the physical plane, I saw only dishonest people; in my invisible brothers and sisters, I presumed I would only encounter deceivers dressed up as guides, and in myself, I feared baneful tendencies. Many friends thought of me as virtuous because of the strictness of my demands; nevertheless, deep down, I was nothing more than a sickly volunteer, burdened with needless afflictions."

"That was very childish of you," retorted the other. "You forgot that in the carnal sphere, the greatest interest of the soul is the accomplishment of something useful for the good of all, something that will last for all eternity. In such an occupation, it is crucial to realize that there will be harassment from all sorts of rival elements. The ironies of ignorance, bouts of unreasonableness, and the menial suggestions of our own animalistic nature will undoubtedly appear on the path of every faithful worker. These are the logical and unavoidable circumstances of our spiritual work, because we do not go to the physical world to take an unwarranted break, but to struggle for our improvement in spite of every unforeseen obstacle."

"I understand that now," said the other. "Nevertheless, the fear of deception jeopardized a wonderful opportunity."

"Ah, my friend," replied Benita, "it's too late for regrets. We're so afraid of being deceived that we end up deceiving the services of Christ."

I was listening to their conversation with growing interest, but my companion led me away to introduce me to new acquaintances.

I was attentive to these pleasant tasks of Nosso Lar society, but so that I wouldn't lose out on an opportunity to learn, I continued eavesdropping on the conversations around me. A few gentlemen were carrying on a discrete exchange of opinions.

"I realize that I failed," said one of them in a serious tone, "and I have already expiated a great deal in the lower regions, but I am waiting for new opportunities from Providence."

"Even so, do you think you lacked sufficient guidance on your path?" asked another friend.

"I'll explain," clarified the first. "I lacked support from my wife. With her at my side, I felt a profound equilibrium in my psychic energies. I can't explain it, but her company compensated for all my expenditures of mediumistic energy. My sense of balance was in the hands of my dear Adelia. I forgot, though, that a good servant must be prepared to serve the Lord in any circumstance. I had not learned the science of compliance, nor had I resigned myself to traveling the human road alone. When I found myself without my dedicated companion, taken from me by death, I became afraid because I felt unbalanced. I wrongly tried to replace her and was harmed. My second wife had a very strong connection to maleficent spirits, and in her derangement she drew me into sexual perversions of which I never suspected myself capable. I unfeelingly went back to fraternizing with perverse people; having started well, I ended badly. My misfortunes were enormous; however, now that I realize my shortcomings, I understand that, even in the future, it will be very difficult for me to prevail without my beloved companion."

The conversation had become extremely interesting. I wanted to follow its progress, but Vicente called my attention to another matter, and I had to join him.

10

Joel's Experience

I accompanied Vicente to a corner of the room, where he addressed a pleasant looking elderly man.

"So, my dear Joel, how are you?" Vicente asked courteously.

Joel replied with a melancholic expression:

"Thanks to the Divine Goodness, I'm feeling much better. I have been going daily to receive magnetic passes in the Aid Chambers at the Ministry of Assistance, and I feel much stronger now."

"Have the attacks of dizziness stopped?" asked Vicente with great concern.

"They're farther apart now, and when they do occur they don't afflict my heart so intensely."

Vicente fixed his very lucid eyes on mine and said with a smile:

"Joel also did mediumistic work in the carnal realm and has a very interesting tale to tell."

Our new friend, who to me looked like a patient just starting his convalescence, smiled sadly and said:

"I made my attempt on earth, but I failed. I was up against a large struggle and I was too weak."

"What impresses me most about his case, though," interjected Vicente in a fraternal tone, "is the malady that followed him here; it persists even now. Joel spent an extremely difficult time in the lower regions. He stayed there for a long time before returning to the Ministry of Assistance, persecuted by strange hallucinations regarding his past."

"His past?" I asked, surprised.

"Yes," explained Joel, humbly. "My role as a medium demanded a more highly refined sensitivity, and when I committed myself to serving in that capacity, I went to the Ministry of Elucidation, where they gave me a special treatment that sharpened my perceptions. I would need to be in a perfect mental state to carry out my future duties. Friendly assistants displayed great acts of kindness on my behalf, and I left for earth with all the requisites that would be indispensable for succeeding in my obligations. Unfortunately, though..."

"But why," I asked, "did you fail in your accomplishments? Was it simply due to your acquired sensitivity?"

Joel smiled and replied:

"I didn't fail because of my sensitivity, but because I used it wrongly."

"What do you mean?" I replied, puzzled.

"My friend, it will be no problem for you to understand this. It's hard to believe, but instead of helping others with such an important gift, I lost myself. The way I see it now, God grants heightened sensitivity as a kind of powerful lens, which its owner must use to discern the best route to take, to determine dangers and opportunities along the way, and to locate common obstacles in order to help his neighbor and himself. However, I did just the opposite. I didn't use my wondrous lens correctly. I allowed myself to be taken by an unwholesome curiosity, and used my 'lens' only to increase my perceptions. Within the context of my mediumistic work, I was able to access past lives. It was supposed to be an indispensable talent given to me for serving the common good and for benefiting my neighbor; however, it was an ability that I did not respect as I should have."

He interrupted his story for a moment, which only increased my desire to hear out his personal experience to the very end. He then continued in the same tone of voice:

"At the first call from the higher planes, I made haste to help. Intuitively, I felt a vivid recollection of the promises I had made in Nosso Lar. My mind was filled with sacred plans. I would work. I would spread the harmony of the eternal truths far and wide. However, as soon as I began my work, my heightened psychic state made the mechanism of my slumbering memories revolve like a record under a phonograph needle, and I remembered everything from my next-to-last existence, when I had donned the cassock under the name of Monsignor Alejandre Pizarro during the final years of the Spanish Inquisition. It was then that I began abusing the sacred lens that I mentioned earlier. The great pleasure of the feelings of power – which can be as harmful as using sense-numbing alcohol – caused me to forget my most-sacred duties. Acute spiritual clarity inspired me. My clairvoyance continued to develop, but I wouldn't be satisfied unless I could once again see my visible and invisible companions from the arena of our former religious struggles. I took it upon myself to find every one of them eventually, making a point of reconstructing their biographical records without any real concern for making the most of the arena of constructive work. My clairaudience became even clearer; nevertheless, I didn't want to listen to my spirit benefactors about beneficial tasks, but instead I insolently questioned them in the *capitulum*[1] of my own selfish satisfaction. Engulfed in investigations concerning the Spain of that era, I wasted an enormous amount of time, during which I fled from fellow spirits who appealed to me to work for the good of my neighbor. I demanded information on bishops, the political authorities of the time, and priest friends who had erred as much as I myself had.

[1] Allegorical reference to the place where church dignitaries meet. – Tr.

"There was no shortage of considerate warnings. Colleagues from our Spiritist group frequently called my attention to serious problems at our center. There were suffering persons who knocked on our door; situations that called for Christian witness. We had a shelter planned for orphans, an outpatient clinic that had just opened, and above all, weekly Gospel lessons on Tuesday and Friday evenings. But what did I care? I cared for nothing but my own personal discoveries. I had forgotten that the Lord had allowed me those memories not to satisfy my vanity, but so that I would understand the extent of my debt to the needy of the world and to hand myself over to the work of enlightening and comforting those who had been wounded by misfortune. Contrary to the expectations of the selfless friends who had helped me to obtain this sublime opportunity, I was not inclined to fraternal cooperation and took no interest in the consoling Doctrine, which is today reviving the Gospel of Jesus among men and women. I only cared about finding those who had something in common with me from the past. With this objective in mind and with unmistakable signs of identity, I discovered I had been connected with eminent personalities in former times. I recognized Mr. Higino de Salcedo, a great landowner who had been my magnanimous protector before the religious authorities of Spain. He was now reincarnated as an intelligent and honest proletarian, but was enduring a major personal sacrifice. I saw old Gaspar de Lorenzo again, a shrewd figure and cruel inquisitor, who had been very fond of me back then but was now reincarnated as a blind paralytic from birth. And in this fashion, my friend, I passed through life from surprise to surprise, from sensation to sensation. I, who had been reborn with the ability to remember past lives in order to construct something useful, had transformed this ability into the corruption of my personality. I lost a blessed opportunity for redemption, and the worst thing is the state of hallucination in which I am now living. As a result of my error in judgment, my mind became unbalanced and psychic disturbances are an ongoing painful torture for me. I am undergoing long-term magnetic treatment."

Just then, Joel suddenly became pale. His eyes opened extremely wide and began wandering as if focusing on impressive scenarios far removed from what we could see. He then staggered, but Vicente quickly caught him, and passing his right hand over Joel's forehead, murmured in a firm voice:

"Joel! Joel! Don't succumb to images from the past! Come back to God's present!..."

I was deeply astonished at seeing that the convalescent, rubbing his eyes, had returned to his normal demeanor.

11

Belarmino the Instructor

The lessons were eminently profitable. They brought me new knowledge, and above all, through them I acquired an increasing admiration for the goodness of God, who was granting all of us the chance to renew our learning experience for future service. Many of us had passed through purgatorial zones of darkness and inner torment; some more, others less. However, all we had had to do was acknowledge our smallness and our immense debt, and there we all were, gathered in Nosso Lar, restoring weakened energies and reestablishing work plans. I could see hope blooming once again in all my fellow spirits. No one felt forsaken. Observing that several mediums were exchanging ideas regarding the panorama of their accomplishments, and hearing so many remarks about instructors, I asked Vicente discreetly:

"For my own edification, would it be possible to learn from the experience of some knowledgeable instructor who might be staying here for awhile? Gathering information and learning from so many mediums would be of enormous benefit and I believe I shouldn't miss out on this opportunity."

Vicente reflected for a minute and responded:

"Let's go find Belarmino Ferreira. He has been my friend for a few months."

I followed him through various groups. We found Belarmino in a corner, talking to a friend. His serious face and slow gestures revealed great sadness in his humble gaze.

Vicente kindly introduced me and an instructive conversation ensued. After exchanging a few ideas, Belarmino spoke with feeling:

"So, my friend, you wish to learn about the afflictions of a failed instructor?"

"Don't say that," I replied mildly, smiling. "I would like to hear about your experience, and also to gain something from your learned words."

Ferreira tried to force a smile that expressed all the remorse still smoldering in his soul, and said:

"The mission of a doctrinal instructor is extremely serious for anyone. It was not without good reason that the title 'Teacher' was attributed to our Lord Jesus. Only since arriving here have I begun to ponder this deep truth thoroughly. I have meditated a great deal, reflected intensely and concluded that for us to attain a glorious resurrection, there is no other path for the time being than the one walked by the Divine Instructor himself. His attitude is worthy of mention because he kept himself from becoming enslaved to earthly assets. In the Gospel, we see the Lord only doing good, teaching love, enlightening people, and spreading the truth. Have you ever thought about that? After many long periods of meditation, I arrived at the realization that in human life, along with those who administer and those who obey, there are those who teach. This led me to the conclusion that in the earthly realms there are stewards, coworkers and servants. Those who teach are primarily of the third category. Do you understand, my brother?"

Ah, yes! I had understood perfectly. Belarmino's appraisal was profound, irrefutable. In fact, I had never heard such beautiful ideas about the educational mission.

After a short pause, he continued, serious as ever:

"It is certainly strange that I failed, knowing so much. My unfortunate tragedy, however, is the same as for all those who know the good but forget to practice it."

He fell silent again, thought some more, and then proceeded:

"Many years ago, I left Nosso Lar with the task of instructing in the area of evangelical Spiritism. My promises before I left here were enormous. My unselfish Elisa prepared herself to accompany me in my toilsome service. She would be my watchful companion, my blessed friend, just as she had always been. My duties would consist of working diligently for the Lord's Gospel, instructing first of all by example, and then by words.

"Two important colonies in the neighborhood of Nosso Lar had sent many to serve as mediums, and they asked our Governor to take part in delivering competent missionaries for teaching and guidance.

"In spite of my guilt-ridden past, I applied for the position with an endorsement from Minister Gedeao, who was most eager to help me. I would perform activities involving my own personal redemption while assisting in the honorable task of bringing light to our brothers and sisters on the visible and invisible planes. Above all, I took upon myself the duty of supporting mediumistic organizations, encouraging my companions-in-struggle, who had been put on earth to serve the immortal ideal. However, my friend, I was unable to escape the entangling web of temptation. From childhood, my parents had helped me with the comforting and edifying ideas of Christian Spiritism. Various seemingly random circumstances led me to become the president of a large Spiritist center. The services offered by the center were promising; its activities, worthwhile and constructive. But led by an excessive attachment to my position as captain of the doctrinal ship, I placed too many demands upon myself. Eight mediums, extremely dedicated to the evangelical effort, offered to collaborate actively with me; however, I sought to place the scientific rule of infallible proof above everything else. I closed my eyes to the law of individual merit, forgot the imperatives of personal effort, and, filled with vanity regarding my own knowledge on the matter, I began to attract individuals of an inferior mental condition to our circle as a result of their enjoying a wrongful position in philosophical culture and scientific research. Strange selfish intentions began to callously flourish in my personal character. My new friends wanted all sorts of demonstrations, and eager to attract collaborators from the field of scientific authority, I forced the poor mediums to make many long forays into the invisible realms. The results were always negative, because each person will receive, both now and in the future, according to his or her own deeds. This really aggravated me. Bit by bit, doubt began to creep into my heart. I lost the peace I used to enjoy. The mediums shrank away from my extravagances, and I began to see them as ill-willed and untrustworthy. Our meetings continued, but I progressed from doubt to deadly disbelief.

"Weren't we a group involved in the interactive exchange between the visible and invisible worlds? Weren't mediums simple devices to be used by deceased communicators? Why wouldn't spirits who could meet our immediate material needs come? Wouldn't it be better to establish a mechanical and rapid process for spirit communications? Why were those on the invisible plane negating my aims to demonstrate objectively the worth of the new Doctrine?

"Elisa tried in vain to call me back to the religious and spiritually edifying realms, where my tormented soul could find relief.

"The Gospel, however, is a divine book, and as long as we remain in the blindness of vanity and ignorance, it will not reveal its sacred treasures. It was for this very reason that I branded it as obsolete. I went from disaster to disaster, and before I could finally settle into my mission of teaching, my esteemed friends from the arena of earth's inferior ways of thinking had dragged me into the depths of utter disbelief. I switched from our Christian group – where I could build an eternal structure – to the realm of politics; not the authentic politics that spiritually edify, but to the inferior corrupt politics that hinder general progress and create nothing but confusion in incarnate spirits. There I remained at a standstill for a long time, sidetracked from my fundamental goals because slavery to money had changed my sentiments.

"And I remained like that until I ended my days with worldly financial success but ... a body riddled with infirmities; with a comfortable 'palace of stone' but a desert in my heart. Since my old inferior nature had resurfaced once more, I was bound again to unworthy fellow spirits both in the incarnate and discarnate realms; the rest, my friend, you can guess: torment, remorse, expiation..."

Concluding, he affirmed:

"But how could it have been otherwise? How can we learn without going to school, without returning to the good and correcting the evil?"

"Yes, Belarmino," I said, embracing him, "you are right. I'm sure that I have come not only to a Messenger Center but to a center of great learning."

12

Monteiro's Account

"The teachings here vary."

It was Belarmino's friend who took over the conversation. Displaying a pleasant speaking voice, he continued:

"I have been coming to the Messenger Center every day for three years now, and there are always new things to learn. I get the impression that the blessings of Spiritism arrived prematurely on the human path. If my trust in the Father were less certain, I would accept such a conclusion."

Belarmino, who was watching his friend's mannerisms closely, interrupted and explained:

"Our Monteiro has a great deal of experience in this matter."

"Yes," he confirmed, "I certainly have had my fill of experience. I too have wandered aimlessly around in various terrestrial settings. As you know, it is very difficult to escape the influence of the environment when struggling in the flesh. The demands of the senses are so many and so great regarding the outside world that I too was unable to escape cruel misfortune."

"How so?" I inquired, interested in increasing my understanding.

"It's that the multiplicity of phenomena and the peculiarities of mediumship hold valuable revelations for any instructor who has more reasoning in his head than sentiments in his heart. At any time, mental corruption can sidetrack any worker who is more enthusiastic than sincere, and that's what happened to me."

After a slight pause, he continued:

"I don't have to explain that I too left Nosso Lar at another time on a mission of spiritual understanding. I wasn't going to induce spirit phenomena, but was nevertheless going to help with the spiritual enlightenment of our incarnate and discarnate friends. It was an immense job. Our friend Ferreira can testify to that fact because we left almost at the same time. I received all the help I needed to begin my grand task, and inexpressible joy prevailed in my spirit as I carried out my first duties. My mother had become my devoted guide and she couldn't contain her joy. Enormous enthusiasm had taken hold of my spirit. I had a number of physical effects mediums under my direct control, as well as some others devoted to psychography[1] and psychophony.[2] The fascination that dealing with the invisible world exerted on me was so great that I became completely distracted from the moral essence of Spiritist doctrine. We held four meetings per week, which I attended with absolute diligence. I must confess that I experienced a certain pleasure in instructing lower order discarnates. I had lengthy, rehearsed exhortations on the tip of my tongue, ready for all of them. I enabled the suffering ones to see that their condition was due to their own fault. I emphatically advised the deceitful ones to abstain from their vicious lies. Cases of obsession earned my impassioned dedication. I delighted in confronting cruel obsessors, reducing them to nothing with my weighty argumentation. Another characteristic that highlighted my strength was the domination I claimed to exert over a few poor, discarnate Roman Catholic priests who were ignorant of the divine truths. I went to the extreme of patiently studying long passages of scripture, not to meditate on them with understanding but to chew on them to my heart's content, and then in the middle of a session and with the sinful notion of false spiritual superiority, spew them out at troubled spirits. My attachment to outward manifestations had completely disoriented me. I lit the torch for others, whereas I preferred the paths of darkness and forgot about myself.

---

[1] Psychography – The writing by spirits using the medium's hand. Kardec, Allan, *The Mediums' Book* (International Spiritist Council, 2006), p. 622. – Tr.

[2] Psychophony – Communication by spirits through the voice of a speaking medium, Ibid, p, 622. – Tr.

Only once back here was I able to see the extent of my blindness.

"At times, after a long indoctrination on patience, for instance, in which I imposed a heavy obligation on discarnates with respect to that particular virtue, I would open the windows of our classroom and harp at the children who were playing innocently in the street. I preached to troubled discarnates to keep calm, but a few seconds later I would scold humble women at the meeting when they were unable to contain their sobs over some sick little child. I acted like that regarding the least little thing; at my place of business my attitudes were just as inflexible. Hardly a month went by when I didn't file a suit over a promissory note. I remember some of the misfortunate retailers who begged me for time, pardon or protection. Nothing would dissuade me, however. The lawyers knew there was no way I would change my mind. I spent my days in the office figuring out the best – but not always the most ethical – way to harass late-paying clients. Then at night I would go to teach love, patience and sweetness to my fellow beings, exalting suffering and struggle as blessed highways of preparation for God.

I was blind. I couldn't see that earthly existence in and of itself is an ongoing Spiritist session. I shaped Spiritism in my own way: every protection and guarantee for myself; valuable advice for my neighbor. Furthermore, I couldn't draw my thoughts away from the phenomena. Apart from the practical sessions, my instructional activity consisted of endless commentaries about these phenomena, wordy duels, stories about uncommon occurrences, and harsh criticism of mediums."

Monteiro paused a bit, smiled and continued:

"I went from error to error, distracted from what was truly essential, when angina caught me completely off guard. I came here like a lunatic needing an asylum. Too late, I realized that I had abused the sublime faculties of speech. How can one teach without setting an example, or guide without showing love? Dangerous and rebellious spirits awaited my exit from the physical plane. I was experiencing an unusual phenomenon: my reason was asking for divine help, but my sentiments were clinging to inferior purposes; my mind was turning to heaven in supplication, but my heart was holding on to the earth. In this sad state, I found myself surrounded by malevolent beings who repeated long passages to me from our former Spiritist sessions. They sarcastically recommended calmness, patience, and forgiveness of others' faults; they also asked me why I didn't let go of the world, since I had discarnated. I yelled, pleaded and screamed, but I had to bear this torment for a long time.

"When my sentiments of attachment to the physical sphere lessened, the commiseration of some good friends brought me here. And just think, my brother, my unhappy spirit was still rebellious. I felt discontent.

"Hadn't I encouraged sessions of exchange between the two planes? Hadn't I devoted myself to enlightening discarnates?

"Realizing how foolishly upset I was, kindly friends committed me to treatment. I still wasn't satisfied. I asked Minister Veneranda for a hearing, since she had been the intercessor for my opportunity as an incarnate. I wanted explanations that could satisfy my personal whims. The Minister is always very busy, but always attentive. She wouldn't schedule a hearing, because of the senselessness of my request; however, out of great courtesy, she visited me during a time she had set aside for rest. I riddled her ears with complaints; I wept bitterly, and for two hours my benefactress – a marvel of evangelical patience – listened to me. In expressive silence, she let me tire of my long and useless exhibition. When I finally shut up, waiting for words that would feed the monster of my incomprehension, Veneranda smiled and replied, 'Monteiro, my friend, the cause of your defeat is neither complex nor difficult to explain. You surrendered yourself excessively to practical Spiritism with humans, our brothers and sisters, but you were never interested in practicing true Spiritism with Jesus, our Master.'"

Just then, Monteiro took a long pause, thought for a few moments, and then spoke, very moved:

"Since then, my attitude has changed a lot. Do you understand?"

Stunned by this profound lesson, I answered, chewing on my words like one who thinks more in order to say less:

"Yes, yes, I am trying to understand."

13

Vicente's Reflections

Even though I had not tired of so many lessons, I had learned enough for now. Impressed by what I had seen so far, I didn't insist on Vicente prolonging our stay at the Messenger Center.

Leaving large groups actively engaged in discussing how they would re-establish their plans and rebuild their hopes, I accompanied my friend, who had invited me to visit the large gardens with him. Enormous rose bushes scented the light and limpid atmosphere.

"I'm really impressed," I exclaimed. "Who would have thought that so many responsibilities could fall to mediums or Spiritist instructors?" I hadn't personally known any such individuals, which explained my current surprise.

Vicente smiled and reflected:

"You, my dear fellow, have come from the Chambers of Rectification, where the duties are very reserved and limited. Perhaps your impression is the result of that situation. You will see in time, however, that there are conversations here involving all sorts of lost opportunities. Have you visited any facility over at the Ministry of Elucidation?"

"No."

"There one can find enormous pavilions that offer schooling on motherhood. There are thousands of sisters there who discuss their misfortunes as failed mothers, seeking to rebuild their energies and plans for becoming mothers again. There are also Paternity Preparation Centers. Large numbers of brothers examine the image of their uncompleted tasks and tearfully remember their past of indifference to their duty as fathers. In that same Ministry there is the Medical Specialization department. Noble medical professionals who lost out on holy opportunities for spiritual growth discuss their problems there.

At that instant, I interrupted and remarked:

"But we are doctors and we're not there."

"Right," Vicente kindly explained. "Unfortunately for both of us, we failed in two of the categories I mentioned. We failed not only as doctors but even more so as men. I might have told you what I suffered through, but I still haven't told you what I did."

"That's true," I agreed, downcast as I recalled my situation of unwitting suicide.

"Also in Elucidation," continued my companion, "there is the Administrators Institute, where educated spirits try to renew their energies and correct the errors they committed during their terrestrial stewardship. In the Work Camps of the Ministry of Regeneration, there are thousands of workers who are renewing themselves to repeat the great job of obedience.

"Those of us who failed at our earthly missions are numerous," he continued, smiling, "and it should be noted that all those who have arrived at places such as Nosso Lar must be regarded as extremely fortunate. Here there are two Celestial Ministries – Elevation and Divine Union – whose sanctifying influence raises the standards of our thoughts without our perceiving it in any direct way. Our training period here, Andre, is a blessing from the Lord, and no matter how hard we work we will never repay a fraction of our debt to this colony. Our situation is that of being sheltered in a veritable paradise because of the edifying service that is offered us. As for our other fellow spirits..."

After a long break, he continued:

"Like so many others, they are going through tumultuous periods of learning in the lowest regions. They are each others' unfortunate prisoners, chained together by remorse and malignant memories. As far as medicine is concerned, countless numbers of our colleagues find themselves in spiritual impoverishment. Human health is a divine heritage and the doctor is its priest. If those who receive a professional title in our area of endeavor do not use it for the good of others, they pay dearly for their indifference. Those who abuse it find themselves, in turn, labeled as criminals. Jesus was not only a teacher but a doctor as well. He left the world the standard of healing for the Kingdom of God. He provided help to the body and ministered faith to the soul. We, however, my dear Andre, do not always relieve bodily ailments in many earthly cases and we almost always kill faith."

My friend's wise words fell upon my soul like rays of light. It was all true, simple and beautiful. I really had never thought about the grandeur of the divine service of Jesus the Physician. He cast out malignant fevers, healed lepers and those blind from birth, and made paralytics stand up – but he didn't stop there. He revived the sick, gave them new hope, and invited them to bask in the sublime understanding of eternal life.

I was engulfed in lofty thoughts when my companion began to speak again:

"I have a friend, a colleague of our profession, who has been in the lower zones for some years, tormented by two cruel enemies. It just so happens that he failed badly both as a man and as a doctor. He was an eminent surgeon, but as soon as he gained renown and general respect, he succumbed to monetary gain and experienced a disastrous fall. During his days of financial big business, he shifted his attention from worthy obligations and set it on the faraway realm of ordinary bankers. If it had not been for spiritual protection, his attitude would have compromised a lot of people's lives. This poor friend nearly lost all his abilities as a doctor. Consequently, a few discarnates, who had been operated on by him, noticed his negligence and blamed their unexpected physical death on him, and so displayed terrible hatred toward him. Friends of the surgeon gave reasonable explanations to many; nevertheless, two of them, who were particularly ignorant and spiteful, persevered in their malevolent attitude and waited for him at the threshold of his tomb."

"How horrible!" I exclaimed. "But if he wasn't really guilty for their discarnation, how can he be tormented like that?"

Vicente explained in a more serious tone:

"It is true that he is not to blame for their deaths. He did nothing to cut short their physical existence; nevertheless, he is responsible for the enmity and incomprehension created in those poor creatures' minds, because, since he was neither certain of his duty nor at peace with his conscience, our friend is deemed guilty due to other wrongs to which he imprudently yielded. All error brings weakness, and that being the case, our colleague has not acquired the strength to disengage himself from his torturers for the time being. Before the divine court, therefore, he is not paying for crimes he actually committed, but is correcting certain egregious wrongs. Moreover, he is learning to know himself, to understand worthy obligations and practice them, and, finally, to understand the happiness of those who are useful, secure in their faith in God and in themselves. The thought of a task well-done, Andre, even when everyone is against us, is a strong light by day and a blessed pillow at night.

Because he abused our profession, our colleague has entered upon a dolorous trial."

"Ah, yes!" I exclaimed. "Now I understand. When there is one wrong, many disturbances may result from it; when we turn out the light, we may fall into any precipice."

"Exactly."

My friend became quiet, walking for some time at my side as if he were as surprised as I was at encountering the avenues of roses. After deliberating for a long time, he invited me fraternally:

"Let's return to the Center. I believe we should hear Aniceto about our regular duties before the day ends."

14

Preparations

When Aniceto came to see us that night, he began by saying:

"Tomorrow we three must leave for an assignment down on earth. Telesforo has recommended a number of important things to do, but I can take care of them myself. Meanwhile, you will both enjoy a week's worth of experience and service."

I was overjoyed. I had returned to my home back on earth on several occasions, going back to the town where I had carried out my last task; however, I had not taken much time to examine the broad potential for fraternal cooperation. Every now and then I had been confronted with difficult situations in which my former fellow citizens were facing important problems, but I felt incapable of effectively helping them to find a desirable solution. I did not have the spiritual techniques for it, nor did I have enough confidence in myself.

Letting me know that he had been listening to these deep, inner thoughts, Aniceto addressed me specially, assuring me:

"You weren't able to help your incarnate friends at those times, Andre, because you hadn't yet acquired the needed capacity to see. But that is reasonable. While in the flesh, we are often inclined to check only for effects without considering their origins. In the beggar we see only indigence; in the ailing person, only a physical breakdown. However, it becomes indispensable to identify the causes."

After meditating for a few moments, he continued:

"Nevertheless, we shall try to remedy the situation. Tomorrow at dawn, you and Vicente are to go to the Magnetic Aid Chamber for Sense Enhancement, which is next to the Messenger Center. I will make arrangements so that you both can acquire the needed improvement in your vision. I would ask you, however, to seek similar help through prayer. Pray that God may grant the expansion of your visual abilities. Be mindfully conscious of the grandeur of this sublime gift, and, above all, send to the Eternal Majesty a thought of consecration to his love and divine service. I do not wish to incite you to unwitting fanatical attitudes. We cannot abuse prayer here, following the corruptions of our earthly sentiments as we once did; that is, in the carnal realm, we were accustomed to using prayer in obedience to capricious fancies, pleading for easy answers that would be detrimental to our enlightenment. But here, Andre, prayer is the individual's commitment to God, a commitment involving witness, effort and dedication to higher purposes. More than anything else, all our prayers should signify a faithful heart. Those in our spiritual condition attune their minds through prayer to the highest spheres, and then a new light shines on all their ways."

In the presence of Aniceto's noble authority, I did not dare speak and even began to fear the possibility that any of my thoughts could be revealed.

With affectionate words of friendship and encouragement, our magnanimous instructor left us.

Vicente and I were reveling in our magnificent plans. For the first time, we would be working on behalf of incarnates in general. Our repose that night was very brief. We were anxiously waiting for dawn so we could receive magnetic aid at the Chamber.

Few times have I prayed with the emotion of that hour.

To begin, the enlightened technicians of the institution established a direct mental relationship with us, and then they submitted us to various spiritual applications, which I am still unable to understand to their full extent and transcendence. I observed, however, that the magnetic work did not take our conscious sense away, and I took advantage of the opportunity for sincere prayer, which was more of a commitment to work than an act of supplication per se.

A while later, we were told we were free to go whenever we wished.

At first I did not notice anything unusual, although I felt new courage and a different feeling of joy in my heart. I felt a sense of well-being in a way that I had not known before. My visual and auditory senses seemed clearer.

Aniceto, who seemed very pleased, was waiting for us at the Center. Our departure was set for noon.

I anxiously waited for the designated time.

We did not leave Nosso Lar like terrestrial travelers, who are generally loaded down with provisions and various bundles.

"Here," said Aniceto jovially, "all our baggage is what we carry in our heart. On earth, it consists of suitcases, bags and packages, but now we must carry purposes, energies, knowledge, and above all, the sincere willingness to serve."

A few traveling companions standing by were laughing with pleasure.

At that moment, our guide made a few recommendations. He assigned colleagues to lead trainee groups, set up work schedules and announced that he would return to the colony daily for a few hours, leaving Vicente and me to work on the earth's surface to perform jobs and make observations that would take the whole week.

Full of hope, we said goodbye to our comrades-in-struggle. This was our first training and work excursion on behalf of our fellow beings.

Just as we were about to set off, our instructor remarked:

"I believe that this journey will be different for you. Of course, you are accustomed to free passage, which is granted by our superiors for our normal work activities. It is also granted to our enlightened brothers and sisters who are on the eve of reincarnating."

"What do you mean?" asked Vicente, puzzled.

"Why, didn't you know? The lower regions between Nosso Lar and the physical realms are so large that they demand a wide, well kept road which needs maintenance just as important earthly routes do. There, physical obstacles cause problems; here, it's spiritual obstacles. The road needs to be kept clear for the essential interchange that must occur. Those who are involved in the duties of our sacred itinerary need to be able to come and go freely, and those who come from the higher spheres to reincarnate must be able to proceed as harmoniously as possible, without direct contact with vibrations from the lowest spheres. The absorption of inferior elements would cause serious imbalances in their rebirth. Such disturbances must be avoided. We, however, are pursuing an expedition of learning and experience. Because of this, we must not give preference to the easiest paths."

Noticing our perplexity, Aniceto ended by saying:

"Let's imagine a huge river separating two different regions. There is one shallow passage that offers a speedy crossing, and there are several passages across deep gorges."

From what our kind instructor was saying, I concluded that he could return to the colony whenever he wanted, and he would not encounter obstacles of any sort anywhere because of the spiritual power that enveloped him; however, he had made himself a pilgrim like us due to of his devotion to the mission of teaching. Vicente and I did not have adequate vibratory elements at our disposal for such great feats. We were commonplace, as were the majority of the inhabitants of our spirit city. We possessed only a few principles of volitation[1]; nevertheless, we were still very far from having acquired it in full. Thus, I had never seen energy and humility so beautifully married. Aniceto was directing us firmly like a strong guide, vigorous and wise, but he had no hesitation in making himself equal to us so that he could serve as a devoted companion.

Meditating on this sublime lesson while in full flight, I watched as the towers of Nosso Lar faded into the background...

[1] A spirit's ability to travel though space. Such an ability is inherent to its moral advancement; i. e. its degree of detachment from matter. (Glossário Espírita at www.osgefic.org). – Tr.

15

The Journey

We made use of our process of rapid transport and had traveled a great distance, when a less beautiful region began to emerge. The sky was covered in thick clouds and something beyond my understanding was keeping us from volitating easily. It seemed like this was not the case with our instructor, however, and Vicente and I had to make a great effort to keep up with him.

Aniceto perceived our problem immediately:

"It might be more suitable for us to use our legs at this point. The atmosphere is becoming very heavy and we aren't very far from Campo da Paz. We don't have to actually go there, but we'll rest at the Rescue Outpost. We will find the resources we need there.

"But what is this place?" I asked, amazed at the profound change in our surroundings.

"We are entering the sphere of stronger vibrations from the human mind. We are still a long way from the earth's surface, but we can already sense the mental influence of incarnate humanity. Great struggles are taking place in these realms and thousands of unselfish brothers and sisters here are devoted to the mission of teaching and consoling those who are suffering. Nowhere is divine help lacking."

By then we had reached the top of a tall mountain enveloped in a vaporous fog. On the ground were various trails laid out like well-formed labyrinths. Noticing our perplexity, Aniceto said optimistically:

"Let's keep moving!"

At that moment – O God of Goodness! – something unexpected caused my heart to leap. In contrast to the darkness, rays of light were streaming from our bodies. My soul was overcome with extraordinary emotion. Vicente and I went to our knees at the same time, bathed in tears, sending our profound thanks to the Eternal in expressions of fervent joy. We were intoxicated with happiness. It was the first time that I had been arrayed in light, light that radiated from all the cells of my spirit body. Aniceto, who had remained standing, watching us with a look of joy, spoke impassionedly:

"Very good, my friends! Let us thank God for his gifts of love, wisdom and mercy. Let us show the Father our recognition. Those who do not know how to thank do not know how to receive, much less how to ask."

Vicente and I remained in prayer for a long time, filled with joy and tears...; then we resumed our journey as if we were dressed in sublime luminosity.

Surprises followed one after the other.

Such pathways were very different from what I had known until then. We were immersed in a strange climate, where cold and the absence of solar light predominated. The topography was a mixture of mysterious landscapes that reminded me of a science fiction movie. High mountain peaks resembled dark stalwart spires defying the vastness. We went down and down, flanking dark precipices in a land of menacing exoticism. Strange vegetation arose from the ground at various intervals between great abysses. Horrifying, frightful birds appeared from time to time, filling the silence with anguished cries. A harsh wind blew all around.

Deeply terrified, I swallowed my feelings and asked our instructor:

"What can you tell us about all of this? I didn't know there were such regions between the earth's surface and our spirit city. I feel as if there is a whole new world in front of us, one totally unknown to me... In deference to you, noble Aniceto, I'm not asking this out of idle curiosity; however, these lands surprise me deeply."

Aniceto, always friendly, smiled kindly and replied:

"This entire world before us here is an extension of our earth. Human eyes can see only a few aspects of the 'valley' as they prepare themselves for real spirit sight.

Likewise, we ourselves can see what humans cannot, but we still cannot see the entire picture.

"This is a different domain, Andre. Human perception can grasp only a specific number of vibrations. Comparing restricted human abilities with the grandeur of the infinite universe, the physical senses are extremely limited. Humans can only receive limited information about the world in which they live. It is true that they have fathomed profound problems with their sciences. Astronomy has shown that the sun is approximately 1,300,000 times larger than the earth and that the star Capella is 5,800 times larger than our sun; it has shown that Arcturus is equivalent to thousands of suns like the one shining on us; it has discovered that Canopus is the equivalent of 8,760 suns like ours, all put together; it has measured the distance between our planet and the moon; it has followed certain phenomena on Mars, Saturn, Venus and Jupiter; it has explored the millions of suns amassed together in the Milky Way; it knows about variable stars, and spiral and diffuse nebulae. And human observation doesn't stop with the unlimited grandeur of the macrocosm. Science has also entered the realms of the atom; it has analyzed the materialization of energy and the movements of electrons; it has studied the bombardment of atoms and has investigated the various corpuscles. But with the aid of high-powered lenses and generators of thousands of volts, all this work is still a service that has only had to do with the outward aspects of life. However, Andre, there are other, subtle worlds amidst the crude ones – marvelous spheres that interpenetrate one another. The human eye suffers from many limitations and all the physical lenses put together wouldn't be able to probe the field of the soul, which demands the development of the spirit faculties in order to be perceived. Electricity and magnetism are two powerful currents that have begun to reveal to our incarnate brothers and sisters something of the infinite potential of the invisible, but it is still too soon for us to claim complete success. Only to the individual with developed spirit senses is it possible for some of the details of the landscape before our eyes to be revealed. The majority of people bound to the earth's surface cannot understand these truths until they have lost their dense physical ties. It is a law that we must not see anything except what we can observe to our advantage."

At this point, Aniceto stopped talking.

Moved by what he had taught us, I kept religious silence.

Suddenly, among the shadows I could make out some black figures that seemed to flee hurriedly, mingling together in the darkness of some nearby caves.

Our guide cautiously gave us a few words of advice:

"Let's try to suspend the luminous effects of our spirit bodies; we only need to concentrate our thought in order to do so. We are going through an extensive region inhabited by many wretched spirits, and a display of our abilities would be an unfair humiliation to those who are suffering."

I took his advice and noticed an immediate effect. The strands of light that had been radiating from my body went out as if by magic. The journey became less pleasant. We descended miraculously down long crags. The darkness became denser; the gale, more mournful and penetrating.

After some time of walking along in silence, we espied a large illuminated castle in the distance. Aniceto made a meaningful gesture with his forefinger and explained:

That is one of the Campo da Paz rescue outposts.

16

At the Rescue Outpost

I was dazzled by the view of the splendid castle! Unable to express the wonder that had overcome me, I walked alongside Aniceto in silence. I was greatly surprised, however, to notice that the magnificent building made use of defenses. Heavy walls surrounded it to a distance that my eyes were unable to reach.

Whoever were to imagine such an institution, located in the invisible zones, would find it difficult to conceive of a fortress of this nature. The notion of heaven and hell, deeply rooted in the popular mind, does not usually allow people to understand the fact that they do not change with physical death, just as a change of residence does not mean a change in personality for the ordinary individual.

I was surprised at seeing our guide ring an almost imperceptible doorbell hidden in the wall. I believe that if Aniceto had been alone, he would not have needed this expedient, given his spiritual power over all rudimentary resistance; however, he had us with him, and once more he strove to be on our level by treating us with dignity. To hide one's own glory is the code of common courtesy in holy and noble spirit societies.

In answer, two servants opened the heavy door, which swung on its hinges just as any door in the oldest buildings on the terrestrial plane would have.

"Hail, messengers of the good!" they both said at the same time, gazing at Aniceto with a reverent attitude.

Aniceto raised his hand, which instantly became luminous, and uttered a few words of love, reciprocating their respectful greeting. We went in.

I was amazed! There was an endless view of wonderful orchards and gardens. The darkness was not so intense here. We felt bathed in twilight softness, thanks to large spots of radiant light. The inside displayed unexpected features. Only now did I realize that the wall hid most of the buildings. Imposing pavilions were nestled there as if we were looking at a prodigious learning institution. Several groups of men and women were performing various functions. No one seemed to notice our presence, because of the interest the work aroused in each one of them.

We followed Aniceto through numerous rows of majestic trees that looked like ancient oaks.

I observed, though, that nature seemed maternal in this blessed Rescue Outpost. The sky was brighter, and the wind was softer, murmuring gently through the abundant groves of trees. Noticing our wonder, our kind instructor explained:

"This peace reflects the mental state of those who live in this resting place of fraternal assistance. We have just crossed a region of great spiritual conflict, which you are still not able to perceive. Nature is a loving mother everywhere, but each place reflects the influence of the children of God who inhabit it."

His explanation could not have been clearer.

The main building was built like a handsome European castle from feudal times. Upon reaching it, we were met by a very pleasant couple.

"My dear Aniceto!" said the gentleman, embracing our guide.

"My dear Alfredo! My honorable Ismalia!" replied Aniceto, smiling.

After warm greetings, he kindly introduced us.

The couple embraced us in a display of cordiality and friendly attention.

"Our esteemed Alfredo," continued Aniceto, "is the dedicated Administrator of this Rescue Outpost. Long ago, he dedicated himself to serving our ignorant and erring brothers and sisters."

"Oh! Oh, please stop!" replied Alfredo, trying to escape the flattering comments. "I simply dedicated myself to my duty."

And as if he wanted to change the subject, he continued respectfully:

"But what a pleasant surprise! It has been many days since we've had visitors from Nosso Lar! It's a good thing you came today, when Ismalia has also come to see me!..."

What? I thought to myself. Wasn't this lovely looking woman his wife? Weren't they living here together as they did on earth? Before I could come to any conclusion, however, Alfredo led us farther inside. The stairs, made from a substance resembling marble, impressed me with their transparent beauty.

From the long, stately veranda, where the columns were decorated with flowering ivy – but very different from the ivy we know on earth – we entered a large hall furnished in old-fashioned tastes. The delicately carved furniture created an enchanting setting. In wonder, I stared at the walls, hung with wonderful paintings. One of them, however, especially caught my attention. It was a huge canvas showing the martyrdom of Saint Denis, Apostle to the Gauls, who, according to my humble knowledge of history, was brutally tortured during the times of early Christianity. Intrigued, I recalled that I had seen a painting completely identical to this one on earth. Wasn't it the famous work by Florentin Bonnat[1], the

---

[1] Leon-Joseph Florentin Bonnat, 1833 – 1922, The Martyrdom of St. Denis. – Tr.

celebrated French painter of recent times? The copy at the Rescue Outpost, however, was much lovelier. The popular legend was beautifully expressed in the finest detail. The glorious, semi-nude apostle, with his head cut off and his torso haloed with intense light, was making a supreme effort to pick up his head as it rolled at his feet while his murderers watched him, overcome with intense horror. From On High, a divine emissary could be seen descending, bringing a crown and palm of victory to this servant of the Lord. In this copy, however, there was profound luminosity as if each brushstroke contained movement and life.

Noticing my admiration, Alfredo said, smiling:

“Many who visit us for the first time enjoy looking at this superb replica.”

“Ah, yes.” I replied, “The original, so they say, can be seen at the Pantheon in Paris.”

“You’re mistaken,” he kindly explained. “Like all other great artistic works, not all paintings originate on the earth. Of course, we owe many sublime creations to the human mind, but in this case the matter is more transcendent. Let me tell you about the true story of this magnificent canvas. It was conceived and painted by a noble Christian artist in a spirit colony closely linked to France. At the end of the last century, the spirit of the great painter from Bayonne, although still bound to the physical plane, visited that colony during a night of exalted inspiration, which as a human he would have simply regarded as a marvelous dream. From the moment he saw the painting, Bonnat couldn’t rest until he had reproduced it faintly as the painting that became famous around the world. But the earthly replicas do not have this one's purity of lines and lighting. Not even this reproduction, however, has the imposing beauty of the original, which I had the pleasure of viewing up close when we were organizing a simple tribute for the honorable visit that that great servant of Christ paid us here at the Outpost. In making the necessary arrangements, I personally visited the spirit city I just mentioned."

Great astonishment gripped my heart. Now I saw the explanation for the holy torture of great artists, who were divinely inspired to create immortal works; now I realized that all high art on earth is sublime because it transmits the glorious vision of men and women in the light of the higher planes.

Appearing interested in completing my thoughts, Alfredo observed:

"With free reign, constructive genius expresses spiritual superiority amidst the sublime wellsprings of life. No one creates without seeing, hearing or feeling, and artists of superior mentality are used to seeing, hearing and feeling the highest accomplishments of the path to God."

But turning affably to Aniceto, he exclaimed:

"Enough digression for now. Let's sit down. You must be tired from your difficult pilgrimage. You need to renew your energies and rest for a bit.

17

Alfredo's Love Story

We took a few minutes to take care of our personal hygiene, and then Alfredo invited us to the table, where Ismalia very graciously asked for various types of fruit to be served.

The two keepers of the castle could not have been more gracious.

Servers came and went with great joy on their faces.

Alfredo's conversation and Ismalia's remarks were filled with interesting and instructive comments.

"And what is your overall impression of the work?" asked Aniceto courteously, addressing our host.

“Excellent, as for the opportunities for accomplishment it offers us,” answered Alfredo in a meaningful tone of voice. “However, I don’t have the same opinion about the ongoing situation. The zones we serve are full of grievous tidings. The present time is one of devastating conflict for humankind, and the combative vibrations that reach us here are of the sort that could weaken any less resolute heart. Discarnates and incarnates are engaged in destructive wars. It’s a shame.”

“Has the number of the needy who seek out the Outpost multiplied?” asked our guide.

“Considerably. Our stores of food and medicine have been completely depleted by the starving and the ill. I have five hundred coworkers, but at the moment we feel incapable of meeting all our obligations. The masses of sufferers are countless. Our landscape used to be free of darkness for weeks on end, but now...”

At that moment, Ismalia asked to be excused from the table. And as Alfredo was gazing at me, I ventured to offer:

“It’s a good thing that you have a selfless companion at your side.”

Alfredo and Aniceto smiled almost at the same time, and the administrator said:

“Ah, my friends! For the time being I do not enjoy the good fortune of having her with me all the time. My wife and I enjoy the divine commitment of eternal union, but I still do not deserve her continued presence. She represents heavenly goodness and I, human reality.”

After a brief pause, he continued politely:

"Aniceto knows our story. You, however, do not. I'd be happy, therefore, to tell you about a few memories. This will have a two-fold benefit: I'll unburden my heart once more by telling of my wrongs, and you two, who will perhaps soon have a new work to do on earth, will certainly gain something from my experiences.

"Ismalia and I safeguarded a small chest of happiness in the world; however, wicked bandits were lurking around our good fortune. My responsibility in the realm of material business was enormous, and because I was far from understanding my sublime obligations as a husband and father, I didn't endeavor to fulfill my rightful duties to my home and to the two little children, whom God had sent into my domestic circle. Ismalia was thus the caregiver of our home. Nevertheless, I forgot that virtue may be tormented by vice at any time, and my noble companion fell victim to the wickedness of a disloyal friend, with whom I had innumerable interests in common in the area of finance. My wife silently endured my wretched associate's pursuit over a number of years, but when he realized the futility of his criminal attitude, out of blatant desperation he sought to poison my unwary spirit. He began by warning me about Ismalia's conduct. He stunned me by surrounding her in false accusations. He bribed our domestic servants and placed spies to follow my dear Ismalia in her tasks as wife and mother. This man exerted a profound influence on me, and due to the ties that bound him and me together, my companion never felt brave enough to accuse him. As I listened to the slander outside my domestic circle, I became intolerable within it. I was unable to regard my wife with the ease and absolute trust of before. I saw evil in her least gestures and sought to discover ulterior motives in her most innocent words. I even started using veiled accusations against her. Ismalia wept but said nothing. Finally, our unfortunate persecutor bribed a man of low status, who, one night, stood next to our bedroom like a common hidden thief, and I was put to the ultimate test. I entered the bedroom in extreme desperation and upon seeing my companion thoroughly at peace, I began to make loud accusations. Fearing I had lost my mind, Ismalia got up, but I didn't listen to her pleas as I searched like a madman for the defiler of my honor... I violently threw open a large old armoire, and ransacked the room. At that moment, the figure of a man stole away in the shadows from the next room, and before I could grab him in my unbridled hatred, he jumped out the window and reached the orchard near our house. Desperately, I ran, shooting at random but to no avail. I went back to the bedroom, and to peak my hateful rage the stranger had left behind a dashing, brand new hat just to accentuate my terrible sentiments. My eyes flushed with anger, and spewing insults, I intended to put an end to Ismalia, who was bathed in tears at my feet; however, something that I never could understand on earth paralyzed my murderous arm. Shouting blasphemies and deaf to her pleas, I left our home, overcome with revulsion. The very next day, I claimed my right to sole custody over my children and arranged for Ismalia, who had turned into a pillar of grief, to be sent back to her father's plantation. I hired a governess for the children, and soon thereafter took a steamship to Europe, where I stayed for more than three years. I never looked for any serious proof, and although my spirit was incessantly tormented, I stifled my innermost sentiments and never sought news of my defamed companion. One day, I received a brief letter from the French coast. A relative provided me with information about my wife. After two years of anguish, caught between homesickness and abandonment, Ismalia had come down with tuberculosis and had died in terrible mental torture. I then decided to return. I settled again in Rio, educated my kids and kept my sorrowful widowhood in the disenchantment of my heart. The years rolled by, one after the other, when I was called to the deathbed of my suffering ex-associate. Facing death, the unhappy fellow confessed his hateful crime and asked for forgiveness, which I unfortunately was unable to give. From then on I turned into an incurable madman. Tired and aging, I meant to go to the rural property of my in-laws to try to repair the injustice in some way, but death did not give me the chance. I returned to the realm of discarnates in a deplorable spiritual state."

At that moment he paused, only to continue with emotion:

"I don't have to tell you that I received all the support I needed from Ismalia. Still, unfortunately for me, we were separated. I didn't deserve the blessing of a sublime union. Ismalia keeps a close eye on me, but she resides on a higher plane, which I must make an effort to reach. For a long time now, I have dedicated myself to the services of our Rescue Outpost, consecrating myself to the ignorant and suffering, and my saintly Ismalia comes here once a month to lift my spirits and support me in my struggles."

"But couldn't she be permanently transferred here?" asked Vicente, as impressed as I was with this moving story.

Alfredo smiled and said:

"I know that Ismalia has worked for it, and that her ideal of eternal union is identical to mine, following the rule that those who are more highly evolved are always in a position to help those who are less so. However, I can't help noticing that she has been advised by our superiors concerning my current need for effort and solitude. I must learn the price of happiness so that I will never again disdain the blessings of God. My wife wants to come down here to be with me permanently, but I must learn to rise to her level, and that is why we have not yet received permission for a permanent spiritual partnership."

Noticing our emotion, he concluded:

"I am expiating impetuous crimes. Because of my sinful impulsiveness, I lost my peace, my home and my devoted companion. As you can see, I didn't kill or rob anyone, but I poisoned myself. Slander is an invisible monster that attacks people through careless ears and unwary eyes."

18

Information and Explanations

Ismalia's return to the circle of conversation kept us from continuing the matter.

Perhaps taking advantage of the opportunity, Aniceto asked Alfredo:

"How do you feel about our continuing our journey now? We thought we might still make it down to the earth's surface today."

Alfredo gave us a meaningful look and said:

"I don't feel I have the right to interfere with your work plans, but it would be better if you spent the night here. Our instruments are indicating the approach of a large magnetic storm for today. Bloody battles are being fought down on the earth and people who are not in the actual line of fire are nonetheless in the line of words and thoughts. Those who are not fighting in the battles of war involve themselves in the combat of ideas by discussing the situation. Very few men and women are striving to cultivate a higher level of spirituality. Thus, it is only natural that all across the planet's surface, thick clouds of mental residue from inattentive incarnates are intensifying, and this in turn increases their afflictions."

Aniceto was listening attentively.

"I'm not concerned about you in particular," continued Alfredo, addressing our instructor, "but I believe these two friends would be in for an unpleasant surprise."

"You're right," agreed Aniceto.

And with a meaningful look on his face, he continued:

"I value the sacrifice our fellow spirits are making in the work of preserving human health."

"They are indeed great workers," said the lord of the castle. "From time to time, I personally observe the centers where they are performing their holy work. Humankind seems to prefer the condition of remaining an eternal child. It builds and tears down the treasures of civilization as if it were playing with dollhouses. Our friends are working very hard so that magnetic storms, invisible to the human eye, do not emit lethal vibrations that would result in the spread of countless epidemics and the miseries of war. The spirit colonies of Europe, especially those of our level, are suffering bitterly to meet everyone's needs. We have already begun to receive scores of discarnates as a consequence of the bombings. Because it is involved in its own mission, Nosso Lar still cannot imagine all the effort that the world conflict has been demanding of our work in the lower realms. The rescue outposts of several colonies linked to ours are overcrowded with Europeans who have discarnated under violent circumstances. We have been notified that prayer petitions from Europe have rent the angelic hearts of the highest level coworkers of our Lord Jesus Christ. Following the terrible bombings of England, Holland, Belgium and France, there were others no less extensive. After our spirit mentors had met several times, they decided to transfer at least fifty per cent of the war's discarnates to our New World centers. In our holding area here, there are more than four hundred."

"But isn't it difficult to rescue such people?" asked Aniceto in a grave voice. "And what about the language issue?"

"Although the rescue work in Europe has been intense, it has been very well organized here," explained Alfredo. "For each group of fifty discarnates, the Old World colonies provide us with one nurse-instructor, with whom we can communicate directly. This way, the problem is not so severe, because our part in this collaborative effort consists only in having to furnish service personnel and relief supplies."

"But wouldn't it be fairer," asked Vicente, "for discarnates of this sort to be kept in the actual areas of conflict?"

Alfred smiled and explained:

"Our highest ranking instructors are of the opinion that such gatherings would be fatal to incarnate spirits as a whole. They would establish pestilential focal points of transcendent origin with unpredictable results. Huge numbers of our brothers and sisters who lose their bodies in the devastated areas are unable to escape from the field of anguish; however, in accordance with our housing quotas, all who show that they are capable of being transferred here are removed from those areas right away so that their tormented thoughts will not weigh too heavily on the vital resources of the stricken regions."

At this point, Aniceto intervened, explaining:

"The countries of the world will return to massacring each other needlessly. The error of one nation will influence all the others, just as the wailing of one man would disturb the contentment of millions. Neutrality is a myth and isolation is a fiction of political pride. Earthly humankind is a family of God, just like billions of other planetary families in the infinite universe. War needlessly causes discarnation en masse, and the individuals who die as a result of war will weigh on the spiritual welfare of the whole earth. As long as there is discord among us, we will pay a grievous price in sweat and tears. War deludes the minds of all peoples, including a large number of centers in the invisible realms. Those who do not take up arms of destruction still use words and ideas of destruction. But all of us will pay our dues. The divine law says that we are to understand and love one another. Everyone will suffer as a result of forgetting that law, but each person individually will be held responsible for the amount of discord he or she has personally brought to the worldwide family."

Alfredo seemed to be seriously contemplating these ideas and remarked:

"That is only just."

Aniceto remarked once again after a longer silence:

"Last week I visited Alvorada Nova, a spirit colony in the higher realms, and I learned that, at the first declaration of war, advanced centers of higher spirituality from neighboring planets established maximum security measures at the vibratory borders they share with us. Our esteemed neighbors have taught us that we must bear on our own shoulders the weight of the entire production of the evil we cause; in other words, we are obliged to do our dirty laundry in our own quarters."

We all smiled at this comparison.

Ismalia had remained silent despite the deep emotion stamped on her face, but she now remarked politely:

"Unfortunately, in the collective sense we are still like the Jerusalem of old, enslaved to error. Every day, Jesus heals us and every day we lead him to the cross. Our deeds are reduced to nothing more than recurring failures. We haven't left the training stage of experience. And unfortunately, we continue to practice politics according to the Caesars, justice according to the Pilates, religious faith according to the Pharisees, priesthood according to the rabbis of the Sanhedrin, belief according the Jairuses (who believe and doubt at the same time) and business according to the Ananiases and Sapphiras. At this step, we cannot foresee the full range of implications of critical events."

Enthused about these explanations, I ventured to say:

"But how atrocious destruction by war is!"

"Yes, but at times like these," Alfredo kindly observed, "prayer is an intense light in the hearts of men and women. It is quite true that the stars shine brighter on moonless nights. You should know that, in order to start making arrangements for receiving desperate discarnates, I have gone more than once to help with assistance work in Europe. A few days ago, some fellow spirits and I went on one such mission to the skies over Bristol. German bombers were flying over that noble English city. The scene of destruction was frightening. In the dead of the night, however, a beam of intense light stood out to our spirit sight. Its rays flashed in the firmament while the bombs hurled to the ground. The head of the expedition suggested that we descend to the source of that luminous beam. I was surprised to find that we were in a church. The sanctuary might have seemed almost dark to human eyes, but it was very bright to ours. Some brave Christians were gathered there, singing hymns. The minister of the worship service was reading the passage from Acts, where Paul and Silas were singing at midnight in the prison, their clear voices rising up to heaven in notes of fervent trust. While bomb fragments were bursting outside, these disciples of the Gospel were singing, united in a celestial vibration of living faith. Our leader told us to remain standing before those heroic souls – who brought to mind the early persecuted Christians – as a sign of respect and recognition. He also sang along with the hymns and told us afterward that city administrators might construct anti-aircraft shelters, but these Christians were building 'anti-darkness' shelters.

"Sometimes," concluded the lord of the castle in a meaningful tone, "it is necessary to suffer in order to understand the divine blessings."

19

Breath

After making some interesting remarks regarding the situation in the carnal realms, Aniceto resumed determining what we would need for our work.

Alfredo amiably offered:

"In light of the imminent storm, you could stay with us for a few more hours, and then be on your way tomorrow at dawn."

And I was deeply surprised when he stated:

"You can use my car until it is no longer feasible. I'll provide a skilled driver and you'll save a good deal of time."

I couldn't hide my wonder. Although I knew about the operations in Nosso Lar by the Samaritans, who used large animal-drawn vehicles in their rescue work in the lower regions, and considering the significant difficulties that we had been faced with on the long journey to the Rescue Outpost, I didn't think it was possible that the institution had such a means of transportation.

I later learned that transportation systems in the zones closest to the earth's surface are based on the transcendent properties of electromagnetism and are more common than one might think.

Our guide seemed to be seriously pondering the situation, and then remarked with concern:

"However, we have urgent work to do in the physical realms. Vicente and Andre need to begin active training."

Alfredo smiled kindly, assuring us:

"Well, you don't have to look any farther. There is always work to be done no matter where one might be. Wherever there is a spirit of cooperation, God's work is also there. Our two friends could work some more with us today in providing assistance. For example, they could accompany us in our prayer work, in which there is always plenty to do and many lessons to learn."

"Excellent suggestion!" exclaimed our instructor. "Individual or group prayer is always a vast reservoir of spiritually edifying teachings."

"By the way," said Ismalia affectionately, "we mustn't delay. It's almost time."

At that moment, as if he had suddenly remembered all the work he had to do, the administrator spoke, addressing his partner:

"Olivia and Madalena need to be advised concerning the provisions that are urgently needed for tonight. We'll require the collaboration of a few more breath technicians. There are quite a few brothers and sisters in a serious state, who have been overcome by stronger physical sensations."

"Breath technicians?" I asked, perplexed, before Ismalia could make any remarks about this type of service.

"Yes, my friend," answered Alfredo attentively, "even on earth, the healing breath is a sublime human privilege. However, while incarnate we are very slow to lay hold of the great treasures that are ours for the taking. Normally, we live there, wasting time on fantasies, believing in futilities or feeding suspicions. Those who could grasp the far reaching implications of this subject could create highly effective breath therapy processes."

"But is such a gift available to any incarnate spirit?" asked Vicente, sharing my surprise.

Alfredo thought for a few seconds and answered respectfully:

"As with magnetic passes, which can be done by a large number of people with noticeable benefits, the healing breath may also be used by most humans with impressive results. However, we must add that at any time and in any situation, individual effort is indispensable. Every worthwhile accomplishment requires serious support. The divine good demands human willingness to manifest itself actively. Our breath technicians were not trained quickly. They practiced for a long time and acquired experience at a high price. With everything, there is a right way to start. They are respected workers because of what they have achieved; they earn significant returns and enjoy enormous veneration, but for all this they must preserve the purity of their words and the holiness of their intentions."

Understanding the interest that his words were arousing, the administrator continued after a brief pause:

"In the physical realms, in order for the breath to be sufficiently established, it is imperative for the individual to have a healthy stomach, a mouth free of evil and accustomed to saying good things, and a righteous mind that is interested in helping. By complying with these requirements, we will have a calming and invigorating breath that is both stimulating and healing. Through such breath, health, comfort and life can be transmitted on the earth's surface as well as here."

And since Vicente and I could not hide our perplexity, Alfredo remarked:

"This is nothing new. In addition to physically touching those he healed, Jesus sometimes touched them with the divine breath. The breath of life runs through all creation. Every sacred page that comments on the beginning of life refers to it. Have you never thought of the wind as the creative breath of nature? As for me, ever since I entered Campo da Paz, where I was sheltered in the worst spiritual condition, I have been learning wonderful lessons on this subject, so much so that in heading this Outpost I have encouraged as much as possible the training of new workers in this area, offering compensation to those who decide to begin this specialized task, which is not always easy for everyone."

Just then, Ismalia greeted some important looking workers, who were getting ready for this task.

Impressed with what I had heard, I closely followed the preparations that were being made.

However, when I was alone with Aniceto once more, I shared my enormous surprise with him, and he answered me in a confidential tone:

"You are forgetting that the Bible itself, alluding to the creation of Adam, says that the Creator breathed on the created form, passing the breath of life to him. Referring to our incarnate brothers and sisters, we must realize, Andre, that even coming from imperfect but good-willed humans, every breath with the intention of relieving or healing is significant because all of us are direct heirs of the divine power. Moreover, it is also necessary to realize that we are not dealing with something exclusive. You yourself spent a short while in our Ministry of Assistance. There is a large department there that specializes in the subject, and where worthy coworkers devote themselves to this type of work. On the physical plane, every mouth with a holy intention can render appreciable aid, but generous and pure mouths can distribute divine aid, transmitting vital fluids of health and comfort."

I was hoping that Aniceto would continue by showing me the magnetic qualities of breath, but Alfredo enthusiastically and eagerly approached us, exclaiming:

"The moment of our assistance and prayer work has arrived!"

"We will follow you with pleasure," answered our instructor, smiling.

We had to stop the lesson and attend to other duties.

20

Defenses against Evil

We descended the steps, and in front of the high walls I could observe the extent of the stately building's defenses. That edifice was much more important than any old castle – it had been transformed into a fortress.

Outside once again, I was able to make out the details of the panoramic view more clearly. I now realized that we had entered through a forward bulwark that highlighted the stateliness of the majestic building. Its general lines stood out distinctly.

I was especially impressed by the fortifications. I saw the message tower, obviously devoted to defense; the pointed bulwark, rising above the moat that allowed for an abundant flow of running water; the watchtower, elegant and imperious. I noticed the patrol road, the cistern, the embrasures, and then the stockades and the barbicans, manifesting the complexity of the entire defensive setup. And the armament? I recognized it in the accouterments installed along the walls – replicas of the small cannons on earth. However, I was moved at seeing at the top of the watchtower an enormous pure-white flag of peace fluttering in the wind like a wide, snowy plume...

The administrator noticed the wonder that had come over Vicente and me.

“I know the impression that our defenses have made on you,” said Alfredo, pausing to explain.

Gazing at us with a very lucid look, he continued:

“Of course, you hadn’t imagined that so much fortification would be necessary here. As you can see, our flag is one of peace and harmony; however, it is crucial to realize that we are performing a duty that must be defended in all circumstances. As long as the universal law of love does not prevail, it is imperative for the reign of justice to persist. Our Outpost has been placed here like a ‘sheep amidst the wolves,’ and although it is not our job to exterminate wild beasts, we must nevertheless defend the work of the good against unwarranted attacks. The organizations of our brothers and sisters who are devoted to evil are extremely vast. Don’t get the idea that they are all ignorant or unaware. The majority of them is made up of the wicked and criminals. They are truly diabolical spirits. Have no doubt about it.”

"My God!" exclaimed Vicente, astonished. "But why do they deliberately organize themselves for evil? Don't they perchance know that the entire universal treasure belongs to the Divine Majesty? Don't they recognize the Sovereign Power?"

"Ah, my friend!" said Alfredo in a serious tone. "I asked the same questions when I arrived here for the first time. The answers I received were incisive and conclusive. We could ask the same questions about earth, Vicente. The criminals who create victims of war, the exploiters of the public welfare, the stingy misers, those thirsty for unjustified dominance, and the vain ones full of foolishness ... they all know, as well as our adversaries here, that everything belongs to God and that the human being is simply a beneficiary of the divine assets. They are not unaware that death called their predecessors to the truth and to account, and that the same road is waiting for them; however, they torment themselves like veritable lunatics, piling up wealth to their ruin and abusing the holiest opportunities. Here you can see the same thing. They want to dominate others rather than dominate their own selves; they make demands instead of giving, and thus they enter into perennial conflict with the divine spirit of the law. Once the duel between their fantasy and the truth of the Father is established, they resist the Lord's corrections and the poor beings transform themselves into true geniuses of darkness until one day they decide to take another course."

Intrigued with his profound remarks, I asked:

"But how do you explain the bases for such an attitude? We can understand such delusion occurring on the earth, but here..."

My generous friend did not let me finish, and continued:

"On earth, our less-than-happy brothers and sisters struggle for economic dominance, for undisciplined passions, and for the hegemony of erroneous principles. Precisely the same thing applies in the zones close to the earthly mind. Among the wicked and ignorant spirits there are cooperatives for evil, economic systems of a feudalist nature, the base exploitation of certain forces of nature, tyrannical vanity, the diffusion of lies, the slavery of those who weaken themselves through negligence, the cruel captivity of failed and careless spirits, passions perhaps more undisciplined than those on earth, sentimental unrest, terrible imbalances of the mind, and anguished aberrations of the sentiments. Everywhere, my friend, spiritual failure is always the same to the Lord, although it varies in intensity and hue."

"But ... what about the weapons?" I asked. "Are they ever used?"

"Why not?" Alfredo promptly replied. "We don't use lead bullets; we use electric projectiles. Naturally, we will attack no one. Our task is rescue and not extermination."

"Nevertheless," I said, deeply impressed, "what is the effect of such projectiles?"

"They are terribly frightening," he replied, smiling, "and above all, they demonstrate the abilities of a defense that surpasses the offense."

"But they only frighten?" I asked again.

Alfredo smiled more meaningfully and added:

"They can cause the impression of death."

"What do you mean!?" I exclaimed with unbridled fear.

The administrator thought for a few seconds, and perhaps pondering the seriousness of his explanation, replied calmly:

"My friend! My friend! Since we are no longer in the flesh, let us seek to discarnate our thoughts also. Individuals here who cling to physical impressions cause their vehicles of manifestation to become denser, in the same way that spirits dedicated to the higher realms purify and elevate their own vehicles. Our projectiles, therefore, expel the enemies of the good by sending out dreadful vibrations, and they can cause the illusion of death by acting on the dense bodies of our fellow beings less advanced on the path of life. Isn't physical death on earth also purely an impression? No one disappears. The phenomenon is merely one of invisibility or sometimes of absence. As for the responsibility of those who kill, that is something else. And beyond this observation, which belongs to the jurisdiction of divine justice, we must also consider the fact that, in this sphere, a modified dense body can reappear every day via the mental matter meant to produce it, whereas to obtain a new physical body, there are souls that sometimes work for centuries..."

Vicente and I kept quiet, stupefied.

Alfredo smiled serenely and asked good-humoredly:

"Do you two know the Hindu legend about the serpent and the saint?"

Before we could say no, Alfredo continued:

"The popular traditions of India say that once upon a time there was a poisonous serpent in a certain field. No one dared pass by there, fearing it would strike them. But one holy man in God's service intentionally sought out the region, trusting more in God than in himself. The serpent struck at him defiantly. He overcame it, however, with a serene look and said, 'My sister, the law prescribes that we do no harm to anyone.' The viper withdrew, ashamed. The wise man continued on his way and the serpent changed completely. It sought out places inhabited by people, desiring to make up for its old crimes. Its behavior was completely peaceful, but from that time on, people began to abuse it. When they realized its complete submissiveness, men, women and children threw stones at it. The unhappy creature withdrew into its den, dejected. It felt afflicted, fearful, depressed. It was then, however, that the saint returned by the same way and decided to visit the serpent. He was amazed to see how far it had fallen. The serpent then told him its bitter tale. It wanted to be good, affable and affectionate, but people persecuted and stoned it. The wise man thought and thought and, after listening to it, answered: "But my sister, there has been a mistake on your part. I advised you not to bite anyone, not to chase and murder, but I did not tell you to stop frightening bad people. Don't attack the children of God, our brothers and sisters on the same path of life, but defend your part in the work of the Lord. Neither bite nor harm, but you must keep the wicked ones at a distance; hiss and show them your fangs."

At that moment, Aniceto smiled meaningfully.

Alfredo took a long pause and concluded:

"I believe the fable needs no comment."

21

Demented Spirits

A very large number of workers accompanied us in our work. Countless scores of individuals were loading large jugs of water, caldrons of soup, and vials of medicinal substances onto several carts.

Going a bit further, I saw that hundreds of spirits were housed together in vast lodgings. With their wandering eyes and sullen faces they looked like a congregation of lunatics in a huge asylum.

Alfredo issued a few orders to a large group of healing-breath technicians, who then left us and headed toward buildings located in a different area.

He kindly explained that benefactors from Campo da Paz had put a large number of infirm spirits there, who were more mentally unbalanced than wicked per se. The patients we were looking at seemed to have improved some. They were walking about and many of them were already conversing with each other despite the mental imbalance they were displaying in their words and thoughts.

Alfredo was explaining the multiple duties of the work routine, when a small group of spirits respectfully gathered around us:

"Alfredo, sir," said an elderly man with a snow-white beard, "I'm waiting for the results of my petition. How are things regarding my lands and slaves? I paid a goodly price to Carmo Garcia. You know that I have been worried about them for many years and I can't waste any more time. When can I go home? I believe you know how much I need to return to my family circle. My wife and children are waiting for me."

As an excellent doctor of the soul, Alfredo was paying close attention to the old man and responded as if he were dealing with a sane person:

"Yes, Malaquias, you are right to complain, but your health will not allow for a speedy return. You know that your wife, Dona Sinha, asked that you receive the appropriate treatment here. I believe that she must have much peace of mind about you. Your thoughts, however, have yet to be put in order, my friend. We still have some more work to do. So why worry so much about your lands and slaves? First your health, Malaquias; don't forget about your health!"

The old man smiled like a patient leaning on the strength and optimism of his doctor.

"I know that what you're saying is right, but my children don't do a thing without me. They're lazy and need me to be there."

But subtly instructing the poor old man, Alfredo objected:

"But where did your children come from to your fatherly arms? Didn't they come from the hands of God?"

"Yes, yes..." agreed the venerable old man, trembling and happy.

"Well, there you go, Malaquias. There are moments in life when we must turn over to God what belongs to him. Furthermore, your children are responsible for themselves, and if they are idle, they will have to answer for the ills they have created around them. For now, it is vital that you renew yourself, clarify your thoughts and calm your heart."

The old man smiled and felt comforted, but before he could speak again, a gentleman of noble bearing stepped forward, exclaiming:

"And the resolution of my case, Alfredo, sir? I feel I have been harmed by untrustworthy relatives. My cousins covet my part of the inheritance from my grandparents. As I already pointed out to you, my cut is larger than the others'. But I heard that the Viscount of Cairu has used all of his influence against me. No one can deny that he is a big swindler. What can't he do with his political shenanigans? He has been poorly informed about me. Have you sent my request to the Emperor[1]?"

"I have sent the message," explained Alfredo with brotherly affection, "and the Emperor will certainly take your request into account."

"But it's been so long!..." the gentleman said impatiently as if he were before a common subordinate.

"But my dear Aristarco," answered the administrator, very calmly, "I believe you are being tested in order to learn about the grandeur of your divine inheritance. What is an earthly heritage worth when compared with your never-ending heritage? Don't think about what you've lost; meditate on the sublime assets you will be able to attain in light of the eternal life. Forget about your ambitious cousins and the Viscount who doesn't seem to understand you. Everything they possess in the transitory realm will have to be left behind when they settle their accounts with the Divine One. Haven't you ever thought about that?"

For a few moments, Aristarco seemed to let loose of his anxiety, and smiling openly he replied:

"That's true! The scoundrels are going to die..."

A woman who seemed distressed stood in front of us and interrupted haughtily:

"Alfredo, sir, I would like for you not to keep me here any longer. My husband is my family's own

[1] Brazil had two emperors, Pedro I and Pedro II, who reigned from 1822-1889. – Tr.

adversary. He promised he would hound our daughters as soon as I was away from home. If I stay here, I'm sure he will squander our assets and corrupt our family name. Please authorize my return. My heart tells me that my daughters are in dire straits. I am more and more convinced that my disease is the result of this state of affairs..."

"I know, my sister," replied our friend with the same thoughtfulness as before. "But what good would it do to return when you are so deeply tormented? Wouldn't it be better to get healed and to ease your mind so that you can help your daughters more effectively?"

"But I don't even know where I am," complained the poor woman, wringing her hands. "I think they've brought me to the ends of the earth to treat a simple fainting spell!"

"Nevertheless, no one is mistreating you," said Alfredo kindly, "and your case is not as simple as it seems. Pull yourself together. Blood ties are spiritually constructive, but above them vibrates the universal family. There are individuals bearing burdens much heavier than yours. Learn to the best of your ability to free yourself from fleeting possessions in order to gain eternal assets."

The unhappy woman did not smile like the others. Shutting herself off in her somber mood, she walked away heavily, eyes blazing with rage as though her mind had been driven far away, incapable of any comprehension.

Other patients wanted to be heard, but the administrator said in a loud voice:

"I cannot assist all of you right now. The day after tomorrow you will be received to hear things explained to you."

And turning to us he explained, smiling:

"In the physical realm, they would all be regarded as completely normal, but here they are true lunatics. They are discarnates who have been clinging to materialistic problems for a long time. They complain and want something done about their individual situations but they fail to grasp the opportunity for illumination. In fact, they disdain it. They accuse others but don't even consider their own mistakes. I have attempted to listen to them to give them an idea of our work in the area of those who are mentally unbalanced because of their excessive focus on inferior purposes. It's not a crime if people are interested in what is occurring on their lands, or if they are concerned about having received an inheritance or if they are concerned about the well-being of their family; however, deep down, the old man who complained about his lands and slaves never thought about anything other than acting like a tyrant in his fields; the gentleman who is waiting for his inheritance wanted to cheat his cousins; and the woman who seemed so interested in her home environment discarnated when she secretly intended to poison her husband. I know their ways, each one of them. They have awakened from a long sleep in unconsciousness and they think they are still incarnate; they also think they can conceal their criminal designs."

I was aghast. Showing my deep astonishment, I asked:

"Have these patients been here for very long? How did they get to the Outpost?

Kindly as ever, Alfredo replied:

"They were brought here in the worst condition. They had been in a deep sleep for a long time and have been gradually recovering their memory until they can be sent to the Magnetic Institutions in Campo da Paz in order to receive better aid and much-needed instruction."

22

Those who Sleep

We continued onward through long rows of sheltering groves en route to huge buildings displaying striking architectural lines.

Although I couldn't explain the phenomenon, the light grew progressively dimmer. What was happening? Vicente and I looked worriedly at each other. Alfredo, Aniceto and the others, however, were walking along unruffled. Their serenity calmed me inside in spite of my insufferable fear.

After walking a little further, we reached another group of pavilions that extended over an area of more than a mile and a half by my calculations. Once we were amongst them, however, the darkness became denser. I was vaguely able to make out what they looked like, and from what I could tell, they were spacious infirmaries with solid roofs, but partially open along their high walls, allowing for the free flow of air.

Dozens of devoted and active workers followed us in complete silence.

Alfredo was the only one to speak. I noticed, however, that he was extremely discreet about what he said.

Everything gave me the impression of having entered a dark cemetery, where visitors were obliged to hold the utmost respect for the departed.

Oddly enough, I noticed that one of the workers had given a small device to Alfredo. He kindly showed it to us, explaining:

"This is a luminous signaling device. We are amidst the pavilions that shelter brothers and sisters who are still asleep. At the moment, there are around two thousand of them here."

The numerous coworkers were moving in orderly fashion toward their assigned service areas.

After a short pause, the administrator said firmly:

"Let's begin the assistance work."

At Alfredo's first luminous signal, several electric lights came on, and then, after having overcome my first impression of horror, I saw long rows of low beds, all of them occupied by individuals immersed in deep sleep. Many had an awful appearance. There were very few whose eyelids were closed in a look of peace. The extreme terror and dolorous desperation of death were stamped on the glazed eyes of nearly all of them. Their faces were covered with corpse-like paleness.

I recalled ancient literature and thought of the old Egyptian tombs. Right there in front of us were hundreds of perfect mummies. Hardly any seemed to be sleeping naturally.

Alfredo approached us and spoke to Aniceto in particular:

"Unfortunately, we cannot assist all of them."

"Why not?" our guide asked, concerned.

"We are waiting for skilled personnel. I have the cooperation of eighty assistants at my disposal for this kind of service; however, each one cannot attend to more than five patients at a time. With that in mind, of the 1,980 patients lodged here, I have separated the 400 most likely to wake up next in order to submit them to intensive treatment.

"And the others?"

"They receive nourishment and heavy medication once a day."

Aniceto was silent and pensive.

Profoundly touched by what I was seeing, I instinctively leaned toward the closest patient and tried to examine his physiological condition. I perceived body heat, a regular pulse and respiratory movement, although I noticed extreme rigidness in his limbs as if he were immersed in cataleptic immobility.

I was overcome by an indescribable sensation. I stood up, frightened, turned to Aniceto as discretely as possible, and asked:

"Explain this to me, for God's sake! What are we looking at here? Are we in some sort of house of death after death?"

My instructor smiled complacently, and explained in a nearly imperceptible voice:

"Yes, Andre, this sleep is truly an advanced picture of death. Under the blessing of this shelter, there are several thousand of our brothers and sisters who are still asleep. They are individuals who never surrendered to the active and renewing good around them, particularly those who were thoroughly convinced that death meant nothingness, the end of everything, eternal sleep. The belief in a higher life is an incessant activity of the soul. Rust attacks the unused hoe. Lethargy invades the spirit devoid of a creative ideal. The men and women who believe in the eternal life even while they are still in the physical realm, and even though they may not be Christians per se, are developing faculties of spiritual movement. They can thus enter the extraterrestrial realms in an animate state, at least in terms of more or less precise locomotion and sense of judgment. However, individuals who persevere in deliberate and complete denial, despite sometimes being affiliated with outward forms of religious activity, are truly unfortunate, because in actuality they see nothing beyond the flesh, nor do they desire any spiritual knowledge whatsoever. Many enter our arenas of service like living embryos in the forever-divine womb of nature. A friend of ours calls them 'fetus spirits'; however, in my opinion, they would be happy if they actually were in that beginning condition. We are certain that many have completely refused contact with faith out of criminal indifference toward the designs of the Eternal Father. They sleep because they have been magnetized by their own negativistic concepts; they remain paralyzed because they preferred narrow mindedness to understanding. Nonetheless, the day will come when they must arise and pay their debts. This is why I regard them as suffering spirits. First, they linger in the sleep they believed in; later on, they wake up. Most of them, however, cannot escape physical and mental illness, just as what happened to those demented brothers and sisters whom we saw a little while ago."

I was greatly astonished. Since Vicente had come closer to listen in, Aniceto explained to both of us:

"Authentic faith is exercise for the spirit. Those who do not exercise their faith in some way on earth, deliberately preferring unwarranted denial, will find themselves unable to move later on. Such individuals need sleep, deep repose, until they wake up to the test of responsibilities that life brings."

Noticing that our guide wanted to avoid a long commentary so that we could follow the assistance work more closely, I stilled the many questions that were burning in my mind.

With the exception of a small group of women who stayed with Ismalia, all the other workers remained in a state of watchfulness at the feet of the mummified groups. Artificial light illuminated the endless rows of beds, but I noticed that none of the patients were reacting to the intense brightness. They continued rigid, corpse-like, prostrate.

I then noticed that Alfredo had begun to work the signaling device in order to send out service orders. Each signal implied a different operation.

I saw that the Outpost workers were in a state of deep silence as they distributed small portions of liquid food and oral medication. Then they gave small amounts of energized water to the unfortunate patients, except for several who seemed ready to receive only broth and medicine. Two thirds of the 400 patients under treatment received magnetic passes. A few others received healing breath applications.

All the work activity was transmitted via luminous signals coming from the hands of the administrator, who seemed interested in preserving the utmost silence. Impressed with what I saw, I asked our guide in a low voice why some of the patients had not benefited from the water and the help of new energies received through passes and the life-giving breath.

Aniceto in all kindness leaned close to my ear with the tenderness of a father calming his anxious little child and said:

"Each one in life, my dear Andre, needs what is specific to them. Here we understand this law of nature to the fullest."

23

Nightmares

While Alfredo continued directing the work, Aniceto received his permission to lead us to some distant beds, on which lay a number of patients who had not been assisted with magnetic aid.

"We need to stress practical experience and take advantage of opportunities when they appear," affirmed Aniceto, smiling."

We followed him curiously while observing the lonely, painful or awful expressions on their death masks.

When we were quite some way from the central area, our instructor explained in a grave tone:

"I would like to determine how beneficial your experience was at the Magnetic Aid Chamber for Sense Enhancement. In order to help our incarnate friends effectively, we must be able to see with clarity and precision."

Pointing to the motionless patients, he added:

"All those who sleep in these pavilions are immersed in bad sleep."

"But in the spirit realms, are there really any who sleep well?" Vicente asked bluntly.

"Of course," replied Aniceto thoughtfully. "In our arena of activity, there are those who enjoy short periods of rest. They are morally upstanding workers who await nightly repose with the peace of mind of those who work and rest with a clear conscience."

He paused as though he were considering the best way to sum it up so as not to waste time, and stressed:

"But such spirits do not need to stay in the emergency facilities of a rescue outpost as do the children of darkness."

Then he returned to the moral of the lesson and continued:

"Those who sleep in turmoil succumb to nightmares. All these unfortunate brothers and sisters around us here seem to be dead, but actually they are prisoners of horrible inner visions. Let's use this to your advantage and proceed with some quick observations. You both used to be concerned with anatomical research, the examination of the viscera and the scientific scrutiny of apparently dead cells; now, you're concerned with the deep auscultation of the soul, the probing of the sentiments, and the examination of the mental realm."

And with a decided expression he concluded resolutely:

"Let's get to work!"

He assigned me to the aged body of a woman:

"Andre, examine this sister in detail. Don't speculate on her outward appearance. Study her with all the ability and insight at your disposal."

I was so interested in heeding his instructions that I didn't even hear the ones he was giving to Vicente.

I tried to forget the outer picture and focused on that female mask with all my mental resources. As I became less and less concerned about other matters, I made out a dark gray shadow that had begun to form over her forehead. The sight seemed to help me concentrate. As I watched the phenomenon intensify, I was no longer aware of any outside object or situation. I was stupefied as I began to discern shapes starting to form within the sphere of that small shadowy screen. A modest house appeared in a humble town. I felt as if I were going through its door. A horrible and agonizing scene was occurring inside. An adult woman, displaying a look of insensitive cruelty on her face, was struggling with a drunken man. "Ana! Ana! For God's sake! Don't kill me!" he was begging her, unable to defend himself. "Never! I'll never forgive you!" yelled the woman, adding in a sinister tone, "You shall die tonight." I saw the unfortunate man collapse, exhausted. "You put poison in my drink!" he shouted in tears. "Forgive me if I have caused you any harm! I'm a father! Ana! My children need me alive! Have mercy! Don't kill me!" She listened coldly and answered hardheartedly, "You shall die even so. I've had the misfortune of loving you, you who belong to another woman! You wouldn't leave her for me, so I shall avenge myself!" Writhing on the floor, the poor wretch replied, "God knows I'm sorry for my sinful past! I want to live for the good, Ana! Forgive me out of love for the Eternal Father! Who Knows? Maybe I could help you like a brother. Help me so that I can help you! Don't kill me! Don't kill me!" The woman, however, as if her malice had been aggravated when she heard his virtuous words, picked up a heavy hammer and shouted, "There is no God! There is no God! You're about to die, you wretch!" And she split his skull with a dull thud. The man died without a scream. Soon thereafter, I saw the criminal pushing the body in a hand cart across a lonely railroad track. I followed her movements with interest. The night was very dark, but I could see her stop beside the railway. She checked the surroundings, made sure no one was looking and deposited her cargo on the tracks. She arranged the body so that the head would be cut off when the train passed, and then she left hurriedly, pushing the small empty cart. I didn't wait for the train. I followed the woman, who seemed uneasy and pensive. However, before she could return the cart to the large backyard, I saw her eyes widen as if she were crazy; she was surrounded by beings that looked like thugs in black clothing. Now it was she who had a strange drunken look of terror. She had overcome a poor, unwary man, but she was about to be overpowered by beings that were perhaps even more wicked than herself. “Help! Help!” she screamed in terror. The scene continued, with the miserable creature spewing out supplications in vain.

I felt like a spectator who needed to do something to help. And thanks to Divine Goodness, I felt nothing for the unfortunate woman but ardent compassion. At the first impulse of revulsion for the crime she had committed, I remembered the lessons I had received in Nosso Lar, and I thought of how I would regard the matter if this criminal were some person dear to my heart. If in the world Ana were by my side, a member of my family, wouldn’t I want to help her? How could I accuse her if I didn’t know anything about her past? Had she received a childhood education, the blessing of a home, the security of untainted affection? Who knows if she hadn’t come from afar like an uncomprehending stone rolling around in the abyss of suffering? What ties might have united her to the victim, who was also deserving of fraternal mercy? How might this sorrowful drama have begun? I didn’t know. I only saw the poor woman surrounded by aggressive shadows as she pleaded for help. I didn’t know how to help her, but I remembered that Ana was my sister, a daughter of the same Father, a sister who had become ill on the common path, although I was unable to determine the cause, at least for now. I was searching within myself for some way to help her, when someone suddenly called to me.

It was Aniceto, who kindly exclaimed:

“Come along, Andre! Vicente and you have been able to make the most of this experience. I’m satisfied. Your thoughts of fraternity and peace have helped this unhappy sister very much. Be assured of it and keep seeking understanding so that you can successfully provide further help. From what you have seen first hand, you now know that all those who sleep in torment here are living strange nightmares that they can't escape for even one minute. We don't need to make comments about any one episode of these lives that were lived in opposition to the Divine Will. All that is needed is to remember that debts, everywhere, follow their debtors."

And with an expressive look, he added:

"Let's return to the center. We need to take part in prayer."

24

Ismalia's Prayer

Within a few moments, we once again rejoined the rest of the group.

The administrator made a luminous signal in the shape of a triangle, and I noticed that all the coworkers stood up in a posture of respect.

"It's prayer time at the Rescue Outpost," said Alfredo kindly to let us know exactly what was occurring.

The sun had disappeared from the sky, but the entire celestial canopy still reflected the golden disc. Twilight tones filled the surroundings with marvelous light effects that were highly visible to us now because Alfredo – although I didn't understand why – had ordered all the artificial lights to be turned off before the prayers. As a result, the darkness became very intense amidst the pavilions, but bathed in sublime tonalities; the sky far above took on a new appearance, and because of that immense illuminated blue roof we had the impression that we were in a marvelous palace.

Deeply impressed, I tried to get closer to the small group of fellow spirits.

Only a few women from the castle's work staff remained with us as though to offer honorable company to the noble Ismalia. The other men and women remained at their work posts not far from the mummified creatures.

I noticed that, although Aniceto had been urged to be the prayer leader, he excused himself, arguing that the position rightfully belonged to Alfredo's devoted wife.

Ismalia, in an indefinably refined gesture, then began to pray, silently accompanied by the rest of us. We followed her plea phrase by phrase, mindful of the recommendations of our guide, who had advised us to repeat each phrase in our own minds in order to impress the maximum rhythm and harmony onto her words – both sound and idea – in a single vibration.

"Lord!" Ismalia movingly began, *"please deign to assist our humble wards by sending us the light of your sanctifying blessings. We are here, ready to do your will, sincerely determined to serve your high intentions. With us, Father, are brothers and sisters still asleep, anesthetized by the spiritual denial to which they yielded while in the world. Awaken them, Lord, if it be your wise and merciful will; awaken them from their sorrowful and unhappy sleep.*

Awaken them to responsibility, to the idea of righteous duty!... Magnanimous King, have pity on your suffering subjects; compassionate Creator, lift up your fallen creatures; righteous Father, forgive your unfortunate children! Let the dew of your infinite love fall on our humble Rescue Outpost!... May your will be done rather than ours, but if possible, Lord, may our patients receive a life-giving ray from the sun of your goodness!..."

Ismalia's voice pierced the depths of my heart.

Watching her for a moment, I noticed that she had been transfigured. Diamond-like lights radiated from her entire body, especially her chest area, whose core looked like it held the glow of a mysterious lighted lamp.

During a brief pause in her prayer, I looked around and noticed that the rest of us were displaying the same phenomenon, although less intensely. Each one of us seemed to display a luminous manifestation to some degree. The women accompanying Ismalia looked almost exactly like her as if they were wearing splendid radiant garments predominated by the color blue. Behind them, Aniceto's light blazed, a surprising lilac color; then Alfredo's light, a soft and subtle green but not too splendorous. Then, behind him were a few workers displaying sublime brilliancy on their foreheads, expressed in a variety of colors; then, Vicente and myself. We displayed a weak luminosity, which nevertheless filled us with intense joy, considering that most of the other coworkers displayed only dark bodies like those in the physical realm.

In a deliberate and moving voice, Ismalia continued:

"Here with us, Lord, are unfortunate mothers who were unable to discover the sublime meaning of faith, falling imprudently into the precipice of sinful indifference; fathers who were unable to overcome materiality during the course of their human existence, incapable of discerning the beautiful mission you had entrusted to them; couples unhappy because they did not understand your kindly and generous laws; youngsters who gave themselves over, body and soul, to the suggestions of illusion!... Many became bogged down in the quagmire of crime, worsening their onerous debts! Now they sleep, Father, waiting for your holy intentions. But we know, Lord, that this sleep does not bring rest to their thoughts... Nearly all of our patients are victims of terrible nightmares for having forgotten your commandments of love and wisdom while in the material world. Although they appear to be immobile, their spirit moves amongst anguishing afflictions that we sometimes cannot fathom. It is they, Father, your wandering children and our companions-in-struggle, who need your fatherly hand to guide their way! Almost all have strayed from the straight and narrow due to suggestions of ignorance, which, like a giant spider, weaves its webs of misery, entangling destinies and hearts! Entreating your mercy for them, we also implore for ourselves the true sense of universal fraternity! Teach us to cross the barriers that separate us so that we may see in each of these unfortunate ones a brother or sister in need of our understanding! Help us to understand so that we may finally lose every impulse to condemn others on the

byways of life! Teach us to love them as Jesus loved us! Lord, we who beseech you here were also spiritual lepers, blind of understanding, paralyzed of will, prodigal children of your love!... In times past, we also slept in the rescue outposts of your mercy!... We are simple debtors, eager to pay off our immense debts! We know that your goodness never fails and we trustingly wait for your blessing of life and light!..."

Ismalia paused again, longer this time. I dried my eyes, damp from sobbing. A gentle warmth, however, swept over my soul. And this new sensation of comfort was so intense that I ceased to focus on myself so that I could look around me. Gazing instinctively upward, I was amazed to see a large quantity of whitish flakes of many different sizes falling copiously on those of us who were praying, but not on those who were sleeping. I had the impression that they were spilling from heaven upon our heads, falling in the same abundance over everyone, from Ismalia down to the least of the workers. I couldn't contain my wonder as yet another phenomenon caught me by surprise. The light flakes disappeared when they touched us, but from our foreheads and chests great luminous bubbles began to fall, which were the same color as the light with which we were covered; they rose into the air and reached the countless mummies. Even then, I noticed the issue of levels among spirits, in that the light bubbles emitted by Ismalia were more brilliant, intense and rapid, reaching many of the patients simultaneously. Next came the ones sent out by the women of her personal circle. After that, came those of Aniceto, Alfredo and the others. The dark-bodied workers emitted weak but visibly luminous vibrations. In that instant of contact with the higher plane, everybody revealed their own worth in the work they could offer.

Noticing my astonishment, Aniceto whispered in my ear:

"In prayer, we encounter the advanced production of power-elements. Although they come from Providence in equal amounts for all those who give themselves to the divine work of intercession, each spirit has a different capacity for receiving them. This capacity is the result of the individual's efforts at striving toward the higher planes. And since God helps humans through other humans, and assists souls through other souls, each one of us can only help our fellow beings and cooperate with the Lord by using the evolutionary qualities that we have already attained in life."

25

Her Prayer's Effects

The lights from the prayer flooded the huge ward. A peace-filled glow now pulsated in everything; it was sweet and radiant, and very different from the artificial lighting. The shiny bubbles that fell from us multiplied in the air as if they were obeying some mysterious process of division. They continued falling on the inanimate and rigid bodies, giving the impression of penetrating their innermost cells.

I was dumbfounded. I had never witnessed phenomena of this nature in Nosso Lar. After all, I concluded, I had received the magnetic aid for increasing my perceptions only a few hours before the journey.

The light grew and spread out in an extraordinary spectacle.

Now, however, we abandoned the meditative posture that we had been using in order to concentrate our strength and to emit our vibratory energies. Nevertheless, our bodies remained enveloped in a huge, radiant sphere. As the overall silence continued, I noticed that the light from the prayer was becoming clearer and more intense. Just as in Ana's case, I began to see that, in addition to their death masks, all those miserable skeletons displayed dark nuclei, which displayed a variety of different forms.

The luminous bubbles continued to fall, but now, as if guided by an intelligent will, almost all of them were converging upon the lifeless foreheads. Then I saw something unheard of and inconceivable.

The mummies (I couldn't think of another label for those sleeping brothers and sisters) began to show signs of life. Some of the wretches began emitting anguishing groans while others, like somnambulists about to wake up, were speaking out loud and describing the nightmares that were tormenting them. Many were moving their feet and hands as if making efforts to flee from their sorrowful sleep.

I was extremely surprised at seeing that two of them, some ways away, had actually gotten up. I remembered them both as having been among those who had received all the treatments that had been offered, including the healing breath. They looked at us from a distance like lunatics who had suddenly awakened, and then broke into a run, horror-stricken, looking like zombies.

I was astonished at seeing that no one showed the least inclination to follow them, and when I instinctively tried to, Alfredo stopped me, exclaiming:

"Don't worry. They would be bitterly surprised if they were informed right now that they had been sleeping for such a long time amongst mummies. They think they're dreaming and it's better that way. They won't be able to get past our fortifications and will ask for help at other facilities, where they'll be received for appropriate treatment."

We remained silent for a few more minutes, and I noticed that the lights were slowly going out as the corpses returned to their previous immobility.

Ismalia announced that our prayer service had ended, and after giving the luminous signal announcing to the workers the end of their duties, the administrator approached us, exclaiming:

"Many thanks for your fraternal cooperation. That was indeed a beautiful intercessory service. No one has gotten up in quite a few days."

Aniceto noticed our perplexity and said to Vicente and me:

"You have seen that prayer work in the material realm is more important than you can imagine. There is no prayer that doesn't receive an answer. And prayer, the daughter of love, is not only supplication; it is communion between the Creator and his creatures, thus comprising the most powerful magnetic influx known. While we are on the matter, however, I might add that evil prayer also has enormous influential potential. Every time a spirit assumes such a mental attitude, a communication link is established between it and the Beyond. If prayer manifests activity in the divine good, then wherever it comes from, it heads toward the Beyond vertically in search of the blessings of the superior life. But we must warn you that evil spirits respond to other evil spirits on the lower planes, and they intertwine mentally with each other. We must stress, however, that every impersonal prayer addressed in the name of God to the Supreme Forces of the Good receives an immediate response. Power elements that vitalize our inner world flow from the highest spheres over those who pray during these blessed tasks, building divine hope within us, and then, in our intense desire to serve with the Lord, they flow outward, saturated with our personal magnetism."

And, attempting to materialize his thought to make it easier for us to understand, he stressed:

"You both saw the elements I'm referring to falling upon us, and you observed their outward flow, carrying the light of each one of us on behalf of our sleeping and suffering brothers and sisters. The Most High granted all of us equal portions of power to help, but we spread it according to our individual ability and coloration. Ismalia, whose sentiments are broader and more universalistic than ours, was able to receive the divine aid more clearly and was able to distribute it more abundantly and effectively. There is a profound lesson in this. As I already said, the Father visits his needy children through the children who seek to understand him. We can't abuse the

Lord the way we abuse our human parents; that is, he does not live to satisfy our personal whims. He would never come in person to dry the tears of the needy who weep as the result of having forgotten the divine laws; those in need must turn to him instead. But the Lord always assists people of goodwill through good people who have been schooled in the divine house of goodness. All our reasonable desires and impulses are answered by the paternal blessings of the Eternal. Even though we may wallow in our tears and afflictions, we are never left helpless. We must only stress that answers from God tend to become greater and more direct to the degree that our merit increases, and we need to realize that for such answers God uses all those who carry the light of goodness within them, or who have merit and confidence to offer aid in his name."

Aniceto's explanations opened up new arenas of meditation for me. My enlightened instructor, though, had not finished the lesson, and after a long pause, concluded:

"Since you have joined me in a course of helpful service, I hope that you will make the most of this moment's lesson. You may have noticed that in these wards there are 1,980 sleeping patients. They all receive regular daily nourishment and medication, but only 400 are being given specialized nourishment and medication because they seem to be more likely to improve. Of these 400, only two thirds have shown themselves capable of receiving magnetic passes. Many cannot receive energized water for now. Very few received the healing breath and only two actually got up, but even so, they were still in a deeply disturbed state. Now that you have begun your work of fraternal cooperation, don't forget this lesson. Let us all do good without any anxiety. Let us sow it always and everywhere, but let us not delay in a demand for results. The farmer can sow his seed at will and wherever he wants, but he must realize that the germination, growth and results belong to God."

26

Listening to the Workers

I noticed that the work at the Outpost was unfolding in the most harmonious and friendly of atmospheres, despite the natural respect for notions of hierarchy.

While we were engaged in lively conversation, Ismalia was involved with several female workers like a real mother, although many of them looked old enough to be her grandmother. Aniceto was teaching us important lessons, drawing upon apparently insignificant circumstances, and Alfredo was welcoming coworkers in every condition imaginable, displaying not just a spirit of solidarity, but one of great kindness. He laughed affectionately or offered opinions without the least sign of impatience or irritation.

That harmonious environment had done me much good. Everything breathed order and understanding, goodness and harmony. I was strongly attracted to the Rescue Outpost administrator's paternal attitude, expressed in energy and friendship, organization and understanding.

I asked permission from our guide to listen to the explanations being given to the numerous coworkers.

I approached, impressed.

At that moment, a friendly coworker was speaking to Aniceto with great interest. He was an elderly man with a humble expression, and was talking to Aniceto with an attitude of true respect.

"Have you heard the news?"

"Yes, Alonso," replied the director unaffectedly, "our messengers have informed me in the greatest of detail. Your widow is still very much grief-stricken, but your little ones are enjoying good health, although they too still feel distressed because of your absence."

The old man, who seemed to be very kind, nodded and added:

"I have missed them so much!"

His eyes displayed a resigned sadness like someone who desires something and measures the extent of the obstacles involved.

"But you, Alonso," continued Alfredo, "mustn't agonize over it. I know that you're now working for your family's future. On earth as parents we can make a lot of arrangements for our children; here, however, we can more safely take certain measures on their behalf. We do not always see things clearly enough to make the right decisions while on earth, but here it is possible to determine more accurately what would be of lasting interest for those we love. The higher sentiment is always the correct path for our soul; nevertheless, we cannot say the same with regard to the sentimentalism cultivated in the physical realm. You must be very careful not to confuse your mind. A longing that hurts and keeps us from attending to the Divine Will is neither praiseworthy nor useful. It is an illness of the heart, casting us into unfathomable abysses of thought."

Alonso stopped smiling and his eyes filled with tears as he spoke in a beseeching voice:

"I realize how appropriate your remarks are, Alfredo, sir. Thanks to Jesus, I have been improving my mental life with the new tasks you have given me, and I feel spiritually renewed, in fact. I know that your words of caution have not been without reason, but I would dare to ask for permission to visit my wife and kids. At night when I'm focused on my prayers, I feel their thoughts around me. They penetrate me deeply and draw all my attention to the earth. Sometimes, I manage to get a little rest, but it's not easy. I know that my wife and children are calling for me in their grief. This certainty disturbs me somehow. I haven't felt the usual steadfastness in my daily work and I would like to remedy the situation. I realize that my current obligations are elsewhere and that I should accept that fact; nevertheless, I must confess that my spiritual struggle has been very great. I'm certain that you'll forgive my weakness. What head of a family wouldn't feel tormented at hearing such anguished appeals from home, and feel helpless at not having the means to assist them as the situation requires?"

And, displaying enormous longing of soul, he wiped his eyes and continued:

"I wish I could urge them to compose themselves and have courage, explaining that my heart is still fragile and needs their support. I would be glad if I could ask them to do just that much so that I could meet my current obligations without failing. Perhaps you'll now give me the permission I need? There's a group of Spiritist friends close to our home ... maybe it wouldn't be hard for me to transmit a few words, no matter how brief, and try to comfort my wife and children!..."

Alfredo remained unperturbed and didn't say no. He seemed to understand completely the concern of the friendly and humble worker. I noticed in his lucid gaze the sincere desire to be of help, and with extreme admiration for his generous conduct, I heard him offer:

"We just might be able to satisfy you, my dear Alonso! Our emissaries could take you there as they make their regular rounds; however, believe me that, as a friend, I would be concerned about you; it might upset your peace of mind. I can't abuse my authority and I know that each one undergoes the experience he needs, but I believe it is in your vital interest to strengthen your soul. It is essential that we conform ourselves to the designs of the Eternal. You and your wife would not have been separated if you didn't need new experiences. Because of your separation from her, you too have been suffering from the difficulties that she has been grieving over in your absence. Alonso, I believe that God leaves us alone sometimes so that we can learn all over again and improve our hearts. When made use of by the soul, however, loneliness precedes the sublime reencounter. Moreover, you must not forget that your children belong to God and that they need to define their responsibilities and think about their own attainments. For now, they are tearful and dejected. Rebellion visits their unwary souls. Domestic chaos set in after you came here. However, what can you do but ask for the blessing of the Eternal for them and for us? They need to accept the way things really are at the moment. You have already given them what was reasonable, and now you too must evolve and grow on the new path to which you have been called. What would happen, my dear fellow, if you allowed a full-scale invasion of unhealthy sentimentalism into your thoughts? You are so dedicated to your family that for now I don't feel you are prepared well enough to see all that has been happening in your old home without suffering disastrously. Some time ago, I authorized the visit of two of our workers to the earth sphere so that they could see their widows and embrace their little ones again. But they were so violently taken aback by the situation that they couldn't return to their duties here. They stayed there, clinging to the nest they had abandoned. They didn't keep proper guard over their hearts. They listened too much to the grieving of their families, enveloping themselves in the heavy fluids of the home environment. After the week that had been granted them was up, they couldn't bring themselves to return.

They were like birds imprisoned by the enticement of temptation. Those in charge of personal news returned to the Outpost without them, which came as a great surprise to me. And frankly, I don't know when they will be able to resume their duties. The damage to both was very great."

After a short pause, Alfredo concluded:

"Flying high requires strong wings."

Alonso, who had been listening wide-eyed, resigned himself:

"I've changed my mind. You're right."

The administrator embraced him and whispered:

"May God illumine your mind."

I was amazed at noticing that other coworkers were approaching Alfredo, begging for explanations and opinions, and I learned much from the example of my administrator friend, who responded to all in a firm and kindly voice in a true display of brotherly interest.

27

The Slanderer

While Alfredo indulged in instructive conversation with a number of his subordinates, Aniceto called us to a small isolated structure and said:

"Time for another lesson."

We moved toward a few chambers that were separated from one another.

Our instructor opened a door to one of them and we saw a madman who seemed deeply irritated. He gave us an expressionless look and screamed loudly. Aniceto, however, approached and greeted him respectfully:

"How are you, Paulo?"

I sensed that his words emitted a certain magnetic flow and the patient showed a profound change. He suddenly quieted down. He was calmer as he sat down, although he was still shaky and skittish.

"Have you been feeling any better, Paulo?" our guide kindly asked, touching him on the shoulder.

At Aniceto's physical touch, the patient seemed more rational and replied:

"I'm getting better, thank..."

Seeing that he had hesitated, Aniceto spoke in a firm tone of voice as if he wanted to help his weakened will:

"Finish it!"

The patient made a tremendous effort and concluded:

"T..h..a..n..k G..o..d."

As I was observing his suffering and indecision, I remembered the patients in the Chambers, to whom Narcisa offered her loving care. Perceiving my thoughts, my mentor explained:

"Do you see the difference between those who sleep, those who are insane and those who suffer? We don't have any of the first kind in Nosso Lar, and most of the unstable ones being treated in Regeneration feel cruel anguish. We must realize, however, that those who are moaning and suffering anywhere are actually getting better. Every sincere tear is a blessed indication of renewal. The mocking, sarcastic or disturbed patients who do not show their pain are more worthy of pity because they remain numbed in a strange rigidity of mind."

And pointing to the sick man in front of us he affirmed:

"Paulo is a patient on his way to real improvement. He still doesn't have a clear awareness of his situation, but he is already weeping and suffering from the memories from his unhappy past."

I listened to his explanation attentively. I remembered that the patients brought daily to Nosso Lar by the Samaritans were indeed suffering tremendously. Those who were not undergoing actual atrocious afflictions displayed a strange fear of the dark. The only spirit whom I observed there and who was completely unaware of her own misery was the poor vampire,[1] who had been refused refuge in the Chambers of Rectification.

Our instructor, with no qualms at all about making the patient a guinea pig, warmly suggested:

"Concentrate your visual abilities on Paulo!"

Encouraged by my previous experience, I focused all my powers of observation on him.

Little by little, his mental screen began to take shape before my eyes. It seemed to be formed of dense nocturnal darkness. I was surprised to see several forms moving about on it and I was astonished as I saw several figures of women emerging. Among them was the figure of

[1] See *Nosso Lar*, chap. 31. – Tr.

Ismalia looking as though she were ill, weakened and anxious. A few desperate looking men also passed by, and I noticed Alfredo himself among them, looking tired and prematurely aged. I heard mysterious voices. Curses and blasphemies rained down on Paulo. The women seemed to be shouting accusations at him; the men looked like ferocious stalkers, hiding in the sick man's strange inner world. However, as I watched the figures of Ismalia and Alfredo moving about on that dark screen, I couldn't contain my curiosity and interrupted my detailed examination to ask our guide:

"How do you explain this phenomenon? I'm aghast!"

But before I could say any more about my overwhelming amazement, Aniceto added:

"I know. You're surprised at seeing Ismalia and her husband in the patient's memories."

And seeing my perplexity, he continued:

"Do you remember Alfredo's story? We are looking at the false friend who destroyed his home. Paulo, however, didn't commit only that disgraceful act, he poisoned the spirits of other women, betrayed other friends and destroyed the joy and peace of other home sanctuaries as well. These desperate memories of the highly afflicted Ismalia and the desperate Alfredo are images created by the slanderer himself to see. Our friends of this Outpost have evolved. They have moved beyond the borders of bitterness and have escaped the monsters of hate. Today they are clothed in light; nevertheless, as punishment for his guilt, Paulo sees them as he imagines them to be. Criminals never manage to escape universal justice, because they carry the crime they committed with them wherever they go. In the carnal realm as well as here, the real landscape of the spirit is that of the inner self. In fact, we will live according to the innermost creations of our soul."

Noticing that I was having a hard time grasping this right away, Aniceto continued after a brief pause:

"For a clearer explanation, let's recall the crucifixion of the Divine Master. We know that Jesus entered into sublime glory after the supreme sacrifice of Calvary; however, we still frequently see him hanging on the cross, martyred by our wrongs and flogged by our whips, because our inner vision compels us to. The condemnation of the Master was a collective crime that will be with us until the day we don the divine light of redemption."

His explanation couldn't have been clearer. I felt I was facing a noble revelation.

"Duty is full of blessings of trust, but debt carries the ghosts of exaction," replied the charitable mentor in a grave tone.

Regaining my composure, I asked:

"But did Paulo come by chance to this Outpost?"

"No," answered Aniceto respectfully. "He was brought here by Alfredo himself, who felt he needed to discipline his own soul. Although our friend is now in charge of this house of love, he disengaged himself from the world under intense vibrations of hate and despair. He suffered greatly in the beginning, although he was never abandoned by his devoted, selfless wife. Alfredo, however, was unable to see Ismalia until he finally managed to disentangle himself from the inferior manifestations of hate. After receiving help in Campo da Paz, he understood what he needed to do. As soon as he had acquired some merit, he interceded for his unfaithful friend, and sought him out in every corner of the abyss. Alfredo so nobly dedicated himself to his self-improvement that he earned the position of administrator of this Rescue Outpost. He brought his ward along with him and currently treats him like a brother. But you mustn't think that Ismalia's husband achieved this spiritual victory just because of the fact that he wanted it; he wanted it, sought it out and nourished it. Now he has it. He has been conversing with Paulo daily for many years. At first, he approached the patient with the need for reconciliation; then, as a charitable person; later on, he gained understanding by comparing their situations; then, he felt compassion, and soon thereafter, sympathy. And now he has achieved true fraternity, the sublime love of a brother for his ex-enemy."

Taking a short pause, he spoke again, enthusiastically:

"As you can see, the teaching of Jesus concerning 'knock, and it shall be opened unto you' is very broad. On the plane of the flesh, we insist on knocking at the door of outward things, looking for favors and advantages. But here, we have to knock at the door of our inner self to find virtue and true illumination."

Vicente, who until now had remained silent, asked:

"So then, will Paulo stay here indefinitely?"

Our instructor made a meaningful gesture and concluded:

"Soon he will return to earth. Ismalia has made innumerable intercessions on his behalf, and when his full reason returns, she does not want him to feel humiliated at having been helped by his own victims. One of the other sisters, the one who was slandered by him, has already returned, and Alfredo's selfless wife has asked her to receive Paulo as her son as soon as the opportunity arises.

28

Social Life

In awe, I observed the sublime sight of the firmament above the Rescue Outpost. The sapphire moonlight enveloped everything. The sky was like an endless, very clear blue blanket dotted with sparkling stars. The afternoon clouds had disappeared.

Contemplating the beauty of the night, Alfredo remarked:

"Fortunately, the magnetic phenomena have moved away from our area. The measuring devices, however, are still registering an enormous conflict of lower energies."

I was about to comment on the beauty of the sky in light of the administrator's remark, when the doorbell rang softly.

There were visitors at the door. Alfredo and Ismalia were both smiling.

The head of the Outpost kindly affirmed:

"Friends from Campo da Paz have come for a visit."

And inviting us to the reception room in the foremost bulwark, he jovially added:

"We enjoy a social life here too. And why not? You have to know how to live."

Delighted with this happy note, I followed the owners of the place. I was speechless when I saw a beautiful carriage drawn by two magnificent white horses. It was a comfortable looking and interesting vehicle, almost identical to the old public carriages from the time of Louis XV, and which I had seen more than once in old publications. A small family from the next colony (which, according to Aniceto, was approximately nine miles from the Outpost) had arrived in it.

Alfredo introduced us all in gentlemanly fashion, except for Aniceto, who was an old friend of the arrivals.

The visitors were the Bacelars and their two young daughters. The head of the group was elderly, but in excellent shape. The woman also gave an impression of maturity, but displayed the same wonderful vivacity as the two young girls.

There was a feeling of great happiness. I didn't observe a single note of undignified conventionalism as I might have on earth. Their gestures, their simplicity, their ease and affectionate words revealed pure sincerity. We were in a social scene inaccessible to falsehood.

Going back inside amongst great displays of family joy, I was informed that the recent arrivals had been friends for a long time and had come to visit Ismalia. The noble lady seemed very content. She had sent invitations to some of the Outpost families, and in a few minutes the castle was receiving crowds of people to take part in the grandeur of the select gathering.

Feeling quite insignificant in the company of these new friends, I confined myself to simply listening and observing.

Soon after the first moments of their private conversation, I heard Aniceto ask Mr. Bacelar:

"How's work going?"

The kindly old man answered with a broad smile:

"Well, always well. We just can't place too much attention on our fellow incarnate spirits."

And he added affably:

"It's essential to learn how to serve and move on."

Our instructor also smiled and observed:

"I understand; I understand. As a matter of fact, human progress isn't a question of mere days. Let's not kid ourselves."

And perceiving that Vicente and I might profit from the conversation, Aniceto pointed to Alfredo's new guest, kindly explaining:

"Our friend Mr. Bacelar is head of the teams that provide assistance to our brothers and sisters in the physical realm. He has long-standing experience with humans and knows them like no one else. You can learn a lot from his observations."

"Not a lot, my dear friend," exclaimed Mr. Bacelar good-humoredly, "not a lot. I am merely a fellow spirit, fulfilling my duties with the help of divine mercy. I can't do a lot, because of my natural deficiencies."

"We're sure that what you have to say will be very beneficial," refuted Vicente, who had been quiet until then.

"Anything you can tell us on the subject of assistance will be a valuable learning experience for us," I said.

Our new friend looked at us knowingly and asked:

"Did you use to be doctors?"

"Yes," we replied at the same time.

Mr. Bacelar thought for a few moments and stated:

"I've always liked talking with my friends by referring to the symbols suggested by their profession. But regarding the activities I myself am involved in, I'm afraid I wouldn't have much to say to two practicing doctors."

"On the contrary," I insisted, "your explanations would enrich our learning experience."

Mr. Bacelar smiled optimistically and stated:

"Don't be so sure. Remember what normal patients are like. Very rarely do they practice preventive medicine. Almost invariably, they wait for the materialization of illness before seeking medical help. They need anesthetics when they go under the knife. They drop their regimen at the first sign of improvement. They stop treatment as soon as the first sign of healing appears. They hate the pain that reestablishes their equilibrium. They dislike to be prescribed purgatives. They prefer medications that taste good. And, above all, they always think they know more than their doctors. This summarizes the way sick incarnate spirits receive and react to treatment while on earth. In our area, however, the aggravating circumstances are more substantial because we are unable to work on the soul in the same way a surgeon operates on a patient's tonsils. We are forced to prepare a suitable mental field in order to sow new thoughts, and then watch for their germination, help the tiny sprouts and wait for time to do its work. Our struggle is not simple, because, although the earth doctor always has loving relatives ready to cooperate on behalf of the patient, we ourselves encounter enormous legions of elements opposed to our restoring and curative activities. In general, doctors on earth offer help to whomever wishes to receive it, at least in situations of grave danger; we, however, often have to offer assistance to those who do not want it, because they are living under veils of profound ignorance."

"You're right," I murmured, hearing such logical comparisons. "Nonetheless, it's comforting to know that there are many fellow incarnate spirits in the world ready to take part in this task."

Mr. Bacelar had a meaningful expression on his face, and said:

"Not always. Cooperation is another problem. The majority of brothers and sisters who offer themselves for service leave the spirit world with promises to fulfill, but they prefer to live a life of ease. Few depart from this common pattern. We rarely find incarnates who are willing enough to love work for work's sake without expecting some kind of reward. Most are looking for instant gratification. In such a condition, they don't realize that their minds have become dark dwellings, overcrowded with useless elements. As a result of their corrupted reasoning, their sight also becomes confused. They see violent storms instead of a heavenly landscape and rocky mountains instead of a path leading gloriously upward. Small delusion by small delusion, they form a continent of immense fantasies. From then on, the recapitulation of their earthly experiences is more strongly inclined toward the animal desires, and when they arrive at that juncture, few return to their sacred duties to consider the grandeur of divine blessings."

Mr. Bacelar paused and then continued:

"And making excuses? In the arena of spiritual assistance, you will someday see how many pretexts are invented by incarnates in order to escape the testimony of divine truth in tasks that are their personal responsibility. The stewards of responsibility allege an excess of duties; the servers of obedience claim a lack of opportunity; the affluent stand guard over their wealth and the poor who have received the blessing of poverty rebel against it. The young say they are too young to cultivate sublime realities, and the elderly declare themselves useless to serve them. Married couples complain about their families, and single people complain that they don't have families. The infirm say they can't, and the healthy say they don't need to. Rarely do incarnates manage to live without contradictions."

Mr. Bacelar seemed willing to continue, but at Alfredo's request, the two young women came to get him and Aniceto in order to try to resolve a private problem that concerned them.

29

Interesting News

Since Aniceto had to leave, Cecilia and Aldonina were left in our company. We immediately struck up a lively conversation. Cecilia had been the Bacelars' daughter on earth; Aldonina was Mr. Bacelar's niece and she was now waiting for her mother to return to set up a home in a nearby city.

Both displayed marvelous mental development, robust intelligence and a notable capacity for expressing themselves.

While the adults were discussing some private matter in another part of the room, Vicente and I listened to these two young women, enchanted by their poise and energy.

I realized that this picture was identical to the social scene on earth; only the sentiments were different because they were genuine. There was not a single hint of anyone putting on a false front. There was pure joy, authentic simplicity and unstained sincerity in everything that was said and done.

As the conversation progressed spontaneously, Cecilia said graciously:

"I've been working for a long time to receive the reward of visiting Nosso Lar. My superiors have promised me the privilege for next year..."

And smiling, she concluded expressively:

"However, I have to meet a few important requirements first."

"Really?" asked Vicente, surprised, "Requirements to meet?"

"That's right," replied the young woman good-naturedly. "Perhaps you are not fully aware of how privileged your current situation is there. Living in Nosso Lar is a great blessing. Have you perhaps not understood that yet?"

We all smiled. And pursuing her line of thought, Cecilia continued:

"According to the instructors who visit us in Campo da Paz, your Ministries are veritable universities for spiritual preparation. The educational opportunity in them is immense. In order for you to appreciate what a blessing Jesus has given you, I believe you would have to live for a few years in our colony, where the ongoing work of watching and assisting others is much more pressing, more demanding."

"But in Nosso Lar, we also have many sufferers. The Ministry of Regeneration is a hive of thousands of them," I objected.

Cecilia, however, revealed a great deal of insight in her remarks:

"Referring to a hive is a good analogy because it implies the potential for work. You should realize, however, that the sufferers who arrive at your colony are already on their way to great achievements. The mentally unstable brothers and sisters there have already felt the torture of the sluggish awakening of their consciences, the remorse and regret that are indicative of renewal. They are sufferers who have been improving steadily because of the positive, elevated environment of the city. Wherever the majority live with kindness, the evil of the minority always tends to disappear. Therefore, Nosso Lar – even for those who weep – has a supreme spiritual advantage."

I was impressed with what she was saying, and offered:

"I myself worked for a while helping out in the Chambers of Rectification."

"I have heard several references to that institution," exclaimed Cecilia, who was knowledgeable on the subject, "but based on what my mentor friends have told me, I hold to my opinion."

And as if she already knew our work procedures, she asserted, smiling:

"There in Nosso Lar, there are many suffering spirits, but in Campo da Paz there are many obsessor spirits. In Nosso Lar there may be many who are still sorrow-laden, but in our arena there are many who are rebellious. It is easier to relieve groaning spirits than to assist rebellious ones. In the Chambers you have mentioned, you correct errors that have already appeared and pains that have already manifested. But here, my friend, we are compelled to struggle with ignorant and perverse brothers and sisters, who are convinced about the dangerous fantasies in which they engage; thus, we must assist patients who do not believe they are even ill."

I had begun to understand the logic of her argument, and realizing that I couldn't counter, the young woman continued, sure of herself:

"Actually, it's quite natural for it to be like that. After all, we are located only a short distance from our incarnate brothers and sisters. And we know that on earth, the situation is no different. How many materialists there disguise themselves as philosophers? How many demons don the robes of saints? How many untrustworthy individuals feign generosity and good intentions? Incarnate humankind's influence on our service center is strong and unavoidable."

Vicente, who had been listening attentively, pondered:

"I realize that there is obviously a large display of sacrifice in all this; nevertheless, the work of Campo da Paz must be highly praiseworthy."

"No doubt about it," replied the young woman. "The founding of the colony is an interesting story. Out of gratitude to Jesus, a group of benefactors decided to organize a colony in his name right in the lower zones. It would function as an institute for the immediate rescue of those in a state of ignorance or doleful guilt, and whom physical death had taken by surprise. The plan earned the Lord's blessing and the colony was founded over two centuries ago. Not all evolved spirits, however, appreciate the work in this ongoing assistance agency. Upon leaving the earth, most victorious missionaries need to renew their energies as a natural right earned because of their faithful work, and high order mentors have their service programs, which they must obediently follow according to the designs of the Lord. Thus, our work is fast-paced, but our results are slow and we have to wait for coworkers to be educated in the colony itself for everyone's benefit. We receive excellent hour bonuses and we are entitled to large intercessory rights, but because of this, we have sizeable responsibilities. We never lack selfless instructors who know how useful those who serve in our colony really are. They come from the higher realms to give us encouragement. Our legitimate requests are never denied, and if resources are slow in coming, our esteemed guides explain the situation so that we do not have to worry while we are waiting for them. So, our group always sticks together, and many prefer to postpone embarking on spiritually uplifting undertakings so that they can remain close to old companions, to whom they are united in unfeigned love."

I was enchanted by the young woman's explanations. Her few statements contained an entire summary of lessons on sacrifice and merit, fraternal commitment and compensatory solidarity.

"Has your family always lived there?" I asked with interest.

The young woman smiled and explained:

"More than fifty years ago, my father was rescued by the Campo da Paz benefactors, and when he had regained his spiritual health, he settled in the colony with an understandable feeling of friendship and gratitude. Later on, my mother joined him, and exactly twenty years ago, Aldonina and I were lovingly drawn there by both of them in order to continue in the family sanctuary. So, we have been working alongside them from the start."

"And do you have many plans for the future?" I asked.

Cecilia made a gesture that revealed the heart of a dreamer, and replied:

"I have many plans and problems to resolve, but I am still waiting for the arrival of someone who is still on earth."

30

In Friendly Conversation

We had returned to our friendly conversation about the beauties of Nosso Lar, when Aldonina intervened to add:

"Some of the members of our family visit your city from time to time. Our sister Isaura, who was married in Campo da Paz three years ago, lives there with her husband, who is an employee in Investigative Services at the Ministry of Enlightenment."

Perceiving our curiosity, she continued:

"He used to live with us, but he was called to work in that department a long time ago. He returned later on in search of his fiancée."

Vicente, who had been anxious to say something, exclaimed:

"We have touched on a matter that has aroused my interest very much since I returned from earth's realms. When I was there, I didn't have the slightest idea about marriage after death. When I attended such festivities in Nosso Lar, I must confess that my surprise bordered on astonishment."

Cecilia, smiling, added spiritedly:

"We felt the same way. However, we must realize that such feelings result from our unhealthy narrow mindedness regarding marriage on the carnal plane. After all, if human marriage is one of the most beautiful acts of life on earth, why should it be any less so here, where beauty is always more quintessential and pure? Furthermore, it is essential to realize that we don't live apart from wise and just laws."

"And how happy are those who marry on our planes!" added Vicente, exposing the secret aspirations of his heart.

Aldonina made an expressive gesture and remarked:

"Yes, for us to enjoy such blessedness here, we must have loved on earth and have been spurred by the noblest impulses of the spirit. To reap such joy, we must have loved with our soul. Those who are dedicated exclusively to their body's desires do not know how to love beyond the bodily form, and are incapable of feeling the deep spiritual vibrations of undying love."

Wishing to turn the discussion back to Isaura, however, I stated out of curiosity:

"Tell us more about the sister who moved to Nosso Lar. I would love to know about her marriage. Cecilia, if you yourself have to wait to be awarded a visit to our city, how did she manage to marry and move there permanently?"

Cecilia smiled and replied:

"That's another story. Isaura couldn't go to her fiancé, because she was in a less advanced state than he was, but since Antonio was more advanced, he could go down get to her. But don't think that the marriage took place without certain preparations or requirements. The groom could go to her and take her to Nosso Lar without any formalities provided he had received permission from the authorities of Nosso Lar. However, one of Isaura's supervisors counseled her on the matter, explaining that as an administrator of a lower level colony, he could not prevent her from going, but he asked her to prepare herself first for six years in Campo da Paz before leaving for good. He wisely added that, in a marriage of souls, it is crucial to purify the hope chest of the sentiments. Our sister had always been very prudent and she accepted his suggestion: she worked for six years in our colony, acquiring cultural values and perfecting her mental field."

I took in this subtle information without hiding my enormous surprise.

"I had already had the honor of visting the couple once," said Aldonina, "when I received a reward for being assiduous and cheerful. I was in Nosso Lar for fifteen unforgettable days; however, although I visited sublime institutions such as the Forest of Waters, the Hall of Divine Art and the Field of Majestic Prayer, I realize I'm far from being fully acquainted with that enormous city. I will go there later, though, because I'm continuing with my work and our instructors have always said that all good things await the destiny of those who know how to serve the good and work with hope."

Admiring the beauty of the young women's sentiments I asked, touched:

"But don't you have similar institutions in Campo da Paz? Aren't there temples of joy open to young people?"

"Ah, yes," murmured Cecilia, like someone who did not wish to seem ungrateful for the Blessings of the Eternal, "the Lord has given us much in our colony; nevertheless, we are in the neighborhood of our incarnate brothers and sisters. The storms that reach us demand our constant attention. The inferior scenes that surround us are deeply sorrowful. Our city doesn't have Ministries of Divine Union or Elevation. We cannot receive higher influences very easily. Our communication and aid work has further need of many people educated in the Gospels in order to be effective. Moreover, it must be in keeping with our objectives. Our colony was founded to offer urgent help. To us, Campo da Paz is more than anything else an advanced nursing center in the midst of all sorts of dangers because ignorant and unhappy brothers and sisters surround our efforts on every side. There are rescue outposts like this one every six miles in the zones of our neighborhood. They act as institutions of fraternal assistance and active sentries at the same time."

The young woman took a longer pause, noticing the effect of her words, and concluded:

"When the work becomes burdensome, our governor has the habit of assuring us that we are on a battlefield but that we have the peace of Jesus within our hearts. No image defines our center as well as that. On the outside, the work is rigorous and unrelenting, but within us there is a tranquility that we ourselves find difficult to comprehend."

"Is your work restricted to the confines of the city?" I asked.

"No, it is multifaceted. Aldonina and I, for example, do a lot of work helping the recently incarnated. Our city prepares an average of fifteen to twenty reincarnations per day and it is absolutely necessary for us to help our fellow spirits or wards, at least during the initial phases of their infancy, which includes their first seven years of corporeal existence."

And perhaps because she read the radiant admiration in our eyes, the young woman added:

"Fortunately, however, our volitation faculties are well developed. We rarely encounter vibratory impediments, and thus we can save a lot of time. Moreover, only our instructors go to work alone. As for us, we venture out only in groups. We need mutual help, not only for the sake of efficiency, but also regarding magnetic support."

And, smiling quaintly, she concluded:

"In the work of assisting others and defending ourselves, we cannot manage without the fair and advanced practice of sincere cooperation."

31

Cecilia at the Organ

When I was incarnate, I rarely had the pleasure of attending such a select gathering.

All the lamps were magnificently alight, and the large trees outside, gently swaying in the breeze, seemed to reflect the moonlight. Graceful couples moved about on the veranda and the long staircases. The castle filled with more and more happiness as the number of guests grew. The administrator was graciously receiving friends from the next colony and was proud at welcoming those who were direct collaborators in his work. Joy shone through on every face, and as I observed the beauty of the scene, I pondered the felicity of social life amongst individuals who had begun to understand and practice "love one another", and who were far removed from hypocrisy and degrading conventions.

We were engaged in lively conversation, when Alfredo invited us to the Music Hall.

There was an overall feeling of happiness. Mrs. Bacelar, arm in arm with the gracious Ismalia, seemed enchanted with the invitation.

We headed to the large room, wonderfully illuminated by soft and shining blue lights. Delightful music soothed our souls. Then, I noticed a choir of child musicians performing a melodious piece, accompanied by a large organ much different from the ones we know on earth. Eighty boys and girls formed a lively, enchanting scene. Fifty of them were playing stringed instruments while the other thirty stood singing gracefully. They were performing a lovely barcarolle (I had never heard anything like it on earth) to marvelous perfection.

Deeply moved, I heard Alfredo explaining:

"The children of the Outpost are our living flowers. They bless us with their fragrance, enchantment and joy, making all our work much more soothing."

We all approached the organ and sat down in comfortable chairs.

When the children finished to warm applause, Ismalia asked Cecilia to play something.

"Me?" said the young woman, blushing. "You have come from the higher realms, where the harmony is sanctified and pure. How could I play anything pleasing to your ears?"

"Don't say that, Cecilia," replied Alfredo's kind wife with a smile on her face. "Uplifting music is sublime anywhere. Go, my child! Remind me of the most beautiful days of home back on earth!..."

And, before the young Bacelar could ask what she would like to hear, Ismalia continued:

"The musical services of the Outpost remind me of our old farm when I would return from boarding school... My parents liked works by the European composers, and I practiced the piano almost every night..."

And resting her moist and shining eyes on Cecilia, she concluded:

"Your mom surely remembers my old and loving father's favorite piece..."

Mrs. Bacelar whispered something to her daughter and we watched as Cecilia walked confidently toward the great instrument. With inexpressible emotion, we listened to her excellent performance of Bach's "Toccata and Fugue in D Minor," accompanied by the jubilant children.

I gazed at Ismalia's face, noticing from the light in her eyes that her thoughts were far away, perhaps at her former home. She discreetly wiped away her tears and embraced Cecilia affectionately when she had finished.

"Now, Cecilia, sing a song from your soul!" said the noble lady with the tenderness of a mother. "Show us your heart..."

Mr. and Mrs. Bacelar were happy and touched. The affection with which they followed their daughter's every movement could be seen in their gestures.

The young woman smiled and turned back to the keyboard, but now she seemed profoundly transfigured: her beautiful face seemed to reflect a different light coming from a higher place. She began to sing in a mysterious, moving way. The music seemed to come from the depths of her soul, immersing us in sublime emotion. I have tried to recall the words of that wonderful song, but it would be impossible to repeat all of them to incarnate souls. The darkness of midnight cannot portray the splendor of the dawn. However, I have remembered a little of it and I will record it as faithfully as I can from my imperfect memory.

As if encircled by a different brightness in which we ourselves were bathed, Cecilia sang in a velvety and caressing voice:

"I have kept for your eyes
The shining stars of the peaceful sky...
I have gathered for your soul
All the pure lilies from along the way!...
My beloved, my beloved,
How long is the journey amidst the obstacles
In this vast ocean of longing
Before the sublime moonlight of eternity!

In vain, the fairy Hope
Lights the light inside me...
Why have you gone to the world like this?!

Return to me, my beloved!
Even though your hands are cold
And your feet are bleeding with pain.

I bring you the relieving balm of tenderness.
Return to me;
Come and breathe once more in the garden
Of immortal union!...

I will heal all your wounds of bitterness;
I will give you direction on your path;
I will love those whom you love
So that you may bless me with your smile.
Return to me, my beloved!
Forget the pain and darkness of the past;
Return once more to our paradise!..."

When she had sung the last notes, I saw her face washed in tears as if bathed in pearls of light. Very moved, Mrs. Bacelar touched Ismalia's hand lightly and said:

"Cecilia has never forgotten him."

Looking extremely touched, Ismalia asked:

"Haven't you received any news of Herminio?"

"The poor thing has experienced one downfall after another," Mrs. Bacelar explained, "and Cecilia knows that she won't be able to count on him for a long time; that is why she is going through such inner torment. However, our daughter hasn't gotten discouraged and she works incessantly, full of hope."

At that moment, however, the young woman, wiping her eyes, returned to her family group.

Alfredo's wife embraced her and said:

"Congratulations! I didn't know that you had progressed so much in the divine art! And what a beautiful song!..."

Cecilia made a timid gesture, kissed the hand of her affectionate friend and replied:

"Forgive me, dear Ismalia, my heart is still very connected to the earth!..."

Ismalia, however, with moist eyes and a full understanding of Cecilia's inner suffering, held her close and murmured:

"To be devoted is not a crime, my good Cecilia. Love is the light of God even when it shines at the bottom of an abyss."

32

A Sublime Melody

In a noble gesture, Aniceto asked Ismalia to perform some musical motif from her higher plane.

She didn't have to be asked twice. Showing extreme graciousness, she sat at the organ and spoke pleasantly:

"This melody is dedicated to our dear Aniceto."

And to our heart-felt wonder, she began her extraordinary performance. From the very first notes, something uplifted me to the sublime. We were silent, enwrapped in ecstasy. The melody, woven in mysterious beauty, flooded our spirits with torrents of divine harmony. A range of the gentlest vibrations had begun entering my heart, when I was suddenly surprised by a completely unexpected impression. With indefinable wonder, I noticed that Alfredo's wife was not singing per se; instead, the sweet music was actually a prayer that bordered on the sublime – a prayer that I *couldn't hear with my ears*, but which I was receiving fully in my soul through subtle vibrations. It was as if the melodious sound were impregnated with the silent and creative Word. The words of praise reached the depths of my spirit, causing tears of inexplicable emotion:

O Supreme Lord of All Worlds
And All Beings,
Receive, O Lord,
The thanks
Of your children, debtors to your love!

Bestow on us your blessing;
Guard our hopes;
Support our convictions
On the never-ending path of life...

May our first thought of love
Be directed to your heart
Each day!

May our joy in living
Be directed to your goodness!...

Father of infinite love,
Extend to us your bounteous and holy hand.

Long is the road
Great is our debt,
But inexhaustible is our hope.

Beloved Father,
We are your creatures,
Blessed rays
Of your Divine Intelligence.

Teach us to discover
The untold treasures
That you have stored
In the depths of our lives.
Help us to light
The sublime lamp
Of the Sublime Quest!

Lord,
We walk with you
In eternity!...
In you we move forever.

Bless our path,
Point us toward the Sacred Accomplishment.
And may eternal glory
Be on your eternal throne!...

May Infinite Light shine from you,
May the sovereign Fount of Love
Flow from your merciful heart,
May the divine breath of eternity sing
In your infinite creation.

May your blessing be
Light to our eyes,
Harmony to our ears,
Movement to our hands,
Impulse to our feet.

In the sublime love of the earth and heaven!...
In the beauty of all lives,
In the progression of all things,
In the voice of all beings,
May you be glorified forever,
O Lord."

What melody was this, heard through indescribable sounds? I couldn't contain my abundant tears. Cecilia had touched our sentiments deeply, reminding us of earthly harmonies and human affections. Ismalia, however, had enraptured our spirits, uplifting us to the Supreme Father. I had never heard a prayer of praise like hers! Furthermore, Alfredo's wife had glorified the Lord in a different way, inexpressible in human language. Her prayer had touched the hidden fibers of my heart, and I realized that I had never meditated on the divine grandeur as I had at that instant, in which a sanctified soul spoke of God with the wonder of her spiritual wealth.

And I was not the only one who was weeping like a child. Aniceto too was wiping his eyes discreetly, and some of the women were raising their handkerchiefs to their faces.

I realized that the prayer had ended because the tone of the music had changed. Its heroic quality had given place to an enchanting lyricism. Enveloped in the profound serenity of our surroundings, I watched as marvelous light poured down from On High upon Ismalia's head, wrapping her in an iridescent rainbow of a magnetic quality, and in enraptured wonder, I saw beautiful blue flowers emanating from the musician's heart and spreading over all of us. They dissolved when they touched us lightly as if made of a bluish mist, filling us with profound joy. Most of them fell on Aniceto, reminding us of her kind words when she had dedicated the song to him. I was deeply impressed by those sublime sky blue fluidic corollas as they continued to multiply around us, penetrating our hearts like petals made solely of colored fragrance. I was feeling so joyful and was experiencing such good spirits that I wouldn't know how to express how I felt at that moment.

A few minutes later, Ismalia finished her majestic melody.

She came down to us, crowned in resplendent light.

Alfredo went to her and kissed her on the face while Aniceto held up his right hand in thanks.

"It has been a long time since I've heard such sublime music as we have heard tonight," exclaimed our smiling guide. "Cecilia has sung of sublime earthly love and Ismalia has enraptured us with divine, heavenly love. It was a wonderful idea to stay at the Outpost. We have also been helped by the light of friendship, which has invigorated our spirits!

The Bacelars approached, deeply moved.

"What marvelous flowers you have given us, dear friend!" said Cecilia's mother as she embraced Ismalia.

"We'll return to work filled with renewed energy!" added Mr. Bacelar, smiling.

The large hall was filled with notes of recognition and sincere joy. Ismalia's melody had been a remarkable gift from heaven. Happiness and enthusiasm were written on every face.

Noticing that Aniceto had withdrawn toward a corner of the hall, I eagerly sought him out. I wanted him to explain the phenomenon of the wordless prayer, the harmonies, the light, the flowers. However, before I could ask my questions, my guide smiled amiably and explained:

"I understand your eagerness," Andre. "You don't need to ask. You were impressed with the spiritual grandeur of our friend's noble companion. I don't have to elaborate. Do you remember Ana, the unhappy creature sleeping in the wards and having cruel nightmares? Do you remember Paulo, the slanderer? Didn't you see that they were bearing heavy mental burdens? Each one of us carries our own personal archives along with us on the paths of life. While evil spirits display the hell they have created within them, the good ones reveal the heaven they have built in their hearts. Ismalia has already amassed many treasures that the moths cannot devour. She can already give of the infinite harmony to which she has devoted herself through goodness and divine love. The light we saw is the same that incessantly pours forth from the higher plane, flooding the paths of life, whereas the melody, the prayer and the flowers were the sublime creation of that sanctified soul. During that moment, she shared with us a part of her eternal treasure! Let us pray to the Lord, my friend, that we have not received such sublime gifts in vain!"

33

En Route to Earth

We still had far to travel, so after resting for a while the next morning, we said goodbye, deeply moved. I, for one, can safely say that I was very sorry to be leaving. I had received such beautiful lessons there!

Alfredo and his wife embraced us emotionally and wished us a happy journey and success in our work.

Several friends from the previous evening also joyfully wished us well.

We took the car and were pleasantly surprised.

I would have a hard time describing that little device. It looked like a small automobile with wings and was propelled by accumulated electrical fluids.

Always attentive, Aniceto explained:

"I agreed to use the car, not because I wanted to enslave you to using less effort, but because our stay at the Rescue Outpost, although brief, proved to be one of the most fruitful opportunities for acquiring the knowledge you still need. You received profound lessons regarding our disturbed and suffering brothers and sisters, as well as regarding the effects of prayer. Thus, our work has taken a big step forward, considering the fact that both of you are involved above all in the task of observing and learning."

And after a short pause, he continued:

"But don't think we can use this car all the way to the earth. I have calculated that we'll only be able to fly it until noon. Then we'll have to continue on foot."

Aniceto fell silent for a few seconds, smiled with a different expression and added:

"But we will have to go on foot only until you have acquired 'spirit wings', which can overcome all vibratory resistance. Such an accomplishment cannot be far off. It will depend on the effort you wish to put forth to acquire them. All who work and cooperate with their mind turned toward God can always expect the best. This is not a promise that I'm making out of friendship. It's the law.

Always air-bound but remaining a bit off the ground, the little car carried us over enormous distances.

Almost exactly at noon, we parked at a humble rest stop used for refueling and repairing that type of machinery.

Our driver said goodbye, wished us a good trip and prepared to return.

Then the landscape became very cold and different. The road we were on was not frightening, but it was very dark and foggy. The atmosphere became heavy, which altered our breathing.

Aniceto gazed with us at the obscure vastness, and spoke in a grave tone:

"Four more hours of walking and we will be on the earth. Watch the shadows around us and take note of the general change. Unfortunately, in most cases, the vibratory emissions of incarnate humankind are of quite a low nature, and these regions are full of dark residue from the mental matter of little-evolved incarnates and discarnates. We will be crossing vast areas that are not exactly frightful, but which look quite dark, nonetheless. Two hours from now, however, we will encounter signs of sunlight."

Quite frankly, our pilgrimage was very heavy and harrowing, and only there did I really perceive the enormous difference between the ordinary road linking the earth's surface to Nosso Lar and the one we were now traveling on foot, whereon we had to overcome great obstacles. I felt moved as I pondered the sacrifice of the great spirit missionaries who help humans; I understood how meritorious their service is and how they need special personal qualities and extraordinary goodwill in order to give ongoing help to incarnate beings.

The monsters that fled at our approach, hiding in the dark background of the landscape, were indescribable, and in compliance with Aniceto's orders, I cannot offer any information about them so as not to create mental images of an inferior nature in the spirit of those who perhaps may read my humble account.

At the time predicted by our guide, we caught a glimpse of the light of the sun once again as if it were early dawn. The spectacle was magnificent and new to me. A mild warmth began to reinvigorate us.

Aniceto gazed at the wonderful sight of the rays of light penetrating the darkness and with eyes moist with tears, he said:

"Let us thank the Lord of Worlds for the blessing of the sun! In physical nature, it is the best image of God we know of. The sun is displayed in the most varied combinations within the solar system according to the substance of the realms we inhabit. The sun shines in Nosso Lar in accordance with the basic elements of life there, while it shines on the earth in accordance with the magnetic qualities of the planet's surface. Furthermore, it appears differently on Jupiter and illuminates Venus with another kind of light. It appears on Saturn in yet another shining garment. Even so, it is always the same, always the radiant seat of our vital energies!"

Deeply moved, we continued on and in a short time the sublime star appeared in the position just before twilight.

On other occasions, the road I was traveling was always lighted and easy to navigate due to my volitation ability, and so I had never had to pay much attention to it. This road, however, passed through dense fog, and I noticed profound differences.

At a certain distance, the earth appeared, not in spherical form (we weren't very far from its surface), but as a landscape interpenetrating the vast regions of the spirit world.

As sunset approached, the sun shone like an enormous golden lamp.

Aniceto seemed extraordinarily happy and exclaimed:

"We have entered the zone that directly influences the earth's surface. From here on, we will be able to practice volitation by using our knowledge of transforming centripetal force. The light bathing us is a result of the magnetic contact between the positive energy of the sun and the negative energy of the planetary mass. Let's keep moving. It won't be long before we enter Rio de Janeiro."

At this point I felt the urge to ask something about direction.

"How will we find our way around?" I asked curiously.

"Before anything else," answered our instructor, "we must not forget that our colonies are situated in the magnetic field of South America. Any compass would work from here on out, but in our case we must educate our minds and find our way around by using the field's unique energy."

We used our volitation ability once again, and shortly the forests of Petropolis came into view. A few more minutes and we were able to observe the major arteries of

Rio. Then, at our instructor's suggestion, we approached the seacoast to take long and deep breaths of air.

Vicente and I were positively exhausted. We realized that the effort had been significant for our scanty energies.

Indifferent to our presence, passers-by hurried along, their minds weighed down with problems of a material nature. Packed buses honked their horns. The great bay seemed full of renewing energies.

When the first electric lights came on, Aniceto invited us amiably:

"Let's take a break! You two look exhausted. I'll show you that Nosso Lar also has some retreats on the planet's surface.

34

Nosso Lar's Support Post

Between 6 and 7 p.m., we arrived at a simple house in a modest neighborhood. On our long trek through the busy streets, I had been extremely surprised by scenes that were completely new to me. I noticed the presence of many low order discarnates following closely behind various pedestrians or attached to them in a strange embrace. Many were hanging from vehicles, and others were watching us from distant balconies. Some wandered around the streets in groups, forming veritable dark clouds that seemed to have fallen suddenly to the ground.

I was frightened. I hadn't noticed these sights during previous excursions to the physical realm. Aniceto, however, explained that the help we had received in the Magnetic Aid Chamber to intensify our visual power had not been useless. We were on a task of active observation intended for our learning experience.

Nevertheless, I could not conceal my surprise. The shadows followed one after the other and I can assure you that, although they were of course invisible to the ordinary person, the number of low order spirits was no fewer than the number of incarnates continuously walking to and fro along the streets. The serenity of Nosso Lar's environment did not exist there, nor did the relative calm of the Campo da Paz Outpost. Unexpected fears settled in my soul and unpleasant inner disturbances assaulted my heart, without my being able to tell where they came from. I had the distinct impression that we had plunged into an ocean of very different vibrations, where breathing was somewhat difficult. Our instructor explained that with time our powers of resistance would expand and that the uncomfortable sensations we were experiencing were because it was the first time that we had descended to the environment of the earth for the purpose of a more intense analysis. He recommended that we remain upbeat and, above all, that we conserve our mental strength in the face of any less-than-worthy scenes that might confront us unexpectedly. In order for help to be effective, he exclaimed, ongoing education is required. It wouldn't be possible to help anyone if we were tied down by weaknesses of any kind.

Aniceto's advice calmed our astonished and uneasy souls, and I did everything I could to adjust to our kindly guide's reminders, especially because he stated that many fellow spirits postponed worthy accomplishments because of unjustifiable fears.

The very humble looking residence we were now approaching gave me a warm feeling of comfort. It was beautifully illuminated by bright spiritual light, which reminded me very much of our city so far away. I was very surprised to see that our guide had paused. Noticing our wonder, Aniceto pointed to the poor house and said:

"This will be our shelter. It is a support post that represents Nosso Lar."

A profound astonishment gripped me inside, but I had no chance for questions. I had to follow our instructor as he headed for the tiny house. We approached the garden that surrounded the very plain building, and I was astonished at seeing that numerous fellow spirits had appeared at the window, waving at us happily.

What could all of this mean? I had visited my hometown and former residence at other times, but I had never seen anything like this.

Aniceto understood my perplexity and explained:

"The brothers and sisters greeting us are spirit workers who have taken up lodging in this tent of love."

A very pleasant and welcoming gentleman opened the door to us.

This was another unexpected detail. Nothing like it had happened when I had gone back to my former home. Its closed doors were not an obstacle to me. Here, however, there was a vibratory sentry system in force that I not known about until now.

Our instructor wrapped our host in a friendly embrace, and then introduced us.

"Here, my dear Isidoro," he said, gesturing to us affectionately, "are our friends Vicente and Andre, new coworkers from Nosso Lar."

"Very good! Very good!" exclaimed Isidoro, giving us a hug. "Our activities need dedicated workers. Come in!"

And he hospitably added:

"This house belongs to all faithful coworkers involved in Christian service."

It was the first time I had seen a spirit with such firm leadership in an earth house.

We entered the modest place.

I was greatly surprised as I surveyed the inside. Physically speaking, there were a few simple pieces of furniture, some old oil paintings on the white walls, an old sewing machine being operated by a young girl around sixteen years old, a boy around 12 years old working diligently on his school exercise books, three children approximately nine, seven and five years old, and as the central figure of the domestic circle, a woman of about forty, knitting a blouse. I noticed, though, that a continuous light radiated from the face, chest, eyes and hands of this woman, which made it impossible for me to suppress an expression of wonder.

Aniceto respectfully pointed to her and said:

"This is our sister Isabel. To humans, she is Isidoro's widow, but to us she is a loyal worker in the activities of the faith."

I noticed that Dona Isabel seemed in some way to be aware of our presence, showing a certain wonder in her look. Aniceto was quick to explain:

"Our friend is a woman of great psychic clairvoyance, but the benefactors that guide our efforts have recommended not allowing her mediumistic faculties a complete view of what is occurring around her. A full divulgence of the spirit environment in which she lives might jeopardize her peace of mind. So, Isabel can see maybe a twentieth of the spirit work in which she is directly involved..."

At this point, Isidoro showed us a small room to the side and spoke to Aniceto in particular:

"Forgive me if I cannot join you in your needed rest. Rest as long as you like, however. I am urgently needed in welcoming other friends."

Our mentor thanked him sincerely, and following him, we came to a humbly furnished room, which was nearly filled with spirits involved in edifying conversation.

Comforting lights shone everywhere. There was an old clock, a large rustic table, a dozen chairs and a few rustic benches.

The overall spiritual lighting, however, was wonderfully effective. Many enlightened and generous individuals from the plane invisible to humans were gathered there. Aniceto greeted the groups that he knew more intimately and introduced us with his usual kindness.

He sensed our wonder, and when we were alone in a corner of the room, he explained:

"We are in a Nosso Lar support post. Isidoro and Isabel set it up in an act of heroism and faith, having left our city for this task over forty years ago. Thank God they both bravely overcame arduous trials, and they courageously kept their commitments regarding their service on earth. Then, three years ago Isidoro returned to our sphere; nevertheless, thanks to his wife's selfless nature and the links of spiritual love they maintain above all physical expressions, they remain as closely united as on the day they first met again in physical life. Because of this unusual circumstance, the authorities of Nosso Lar granted him permission to stay on at the house as a loving husband, devoted father, vigilant guard and faithful worker."

Perhaps observing our even greater wonder, Aniceto added:

"No, friends, chance does not define responsibilities, nor does it lend itself to serious commitments. Spiritual edification requires effort and dedication. Just as the ships of the world need firm anchors while they are being unloaded in port, we need courageous and selfless brothers and sisters who fulfill the role of anchors among incarnate beings so that the great benefactors from the higher spirit realms can make themselves felt among humans who are still animalistic, ignorant and unhappy."

35

Home Worship

In the early hours of evening, Dona Isabel left her needlepoint and invited the little ones to the home worship service.

Noting the interest that the children had sparked in me, Aniceto explained:

"The little girls are friends from Nosso Lar, who have reincarnated for spiritual work and redemption. The same is not true of the little boy, however. He has come from a lower region of the spirit world."

In fact, I had perceived the situation exactly. The boy was not clothed in luminous substance and accepted his mother's invitation not as one who is happy to do so, but as one who is simply obeying orders.

They all sat so naturally around the table that I perceived that this blessed family custom had been a long-standing practice in the home. The oldest child, Joaninha, brought notebooks and newspaper clippings.

The widow sat at the head of the table, and after meditating for a few moments, she asked little nine-year-old Neli to say the opening prayer, asking Jesus for spiritual enlightenment.

All the invisible workers sat down respectfully. Isidoro and a few of the couple's closest friends sat next to Dona Isabel; nearly all of them could be seen and heard by her.

As soon as the worship service began, the background lighting became more intense.

A deep sense of peace enveloped my heart.

Little Neli said the prayer in a moving voice:

"Lord, may your will be done on earth as it is in heaven. If it is your holy plan for us to receive more light, then enable us, Lord, to gain more understanding from this gospel study! Give us bread for our souls and the water of eternal life! Be in our hearts, now and forever. Amen!..."

Dona Isabel asked her oldest daughter to read some instructive and comforting words, and then something interesting from the regular news. Joaninha did so, reading a short chapter from an instructional Spiritist book about imprudence and then a sad event from the secular newspaper. Isidoro's firstborn, a very sweet and affable girl, looked quite upset. The clipping was about a young girl in a distant neighborhood who had committed suicide. The reporter had described the scene in graphic detail. Joaninha trembled, grief-stricken.

As soon as she had finished, Dona Isabel opened the New Testament *as if* at random, but I saw that, on our plane, Isidoro was in fact intervening in the process, influencing the topic that was to be focused on that evening. Then she gazed at the small page and said:

"The verse for today, my children, is from chapter 13 of the Gospel of St. Matthew."

She read verse 31 out loud:

"He told another parable to them, saying, 'The kingdom of heaven is like a mustard seed, which a man took and sowed in his field.'"

I then witnessed an interesting incident. A spirit friend, whom I recognized to be of a very high order by his resplendent apparel, placed his right hand on the selfless widow's forehead.

Before I could ask him, Aniceto explained in an almost inaudible voice:

"That is our brother Fabio Aleto. He is going to give the spiritual interpretation of the text. Those who are at his level will be able to *hear his thoughts*, but those who are in a lower mental zone will receive an interpretation of it, as will the incarnates; in other words, we will receive the spiritual light of Fabio's words in the translation of Isabel's materialized words."

Our mentor could not have been more explicit. He had summed up the complex lesson in only a few words.

I noticed that Isidoro's widow had entered into deep concentration for a few moments as if she were absorbing the light encircling her. Then, with an extraordinarily firm gaze, she began her commentary:

"My children, today we have read some words about imprudence and a news item about a suicide under very sad circumstances. The newspaper clipping states that the young girl killed herself because she was so much in love; however, from what we have been learning, we know that no one commits a wrong out of true love. Those who truly love are cultivators of life; they never spread death. The poor girl was ill, disturbed, and imprudent. She gave into passion, which confounds the reason and debases the sentiments. And we know that it is only a small step from passion to suffering or death. However, let's remember this unknown friend with thoughts of fraternal sympathy. May Jesus protect her on new paths. We are not criticizing an act, which only the Lord can judge, but a fact, from which we must extract the right lesson.

"The gospel message this evening – the word of our divine Master to his disciples – affirms that the kingdom of heaven is like a mustard seed, which a man took and sowed in the field of his heart. We must see in this action, my children, a lesson about the smallest things. The physical realm where we live is filled with imprudence of every sort. Few people have begun to reflect seriously about life and duty before they are on their deathbed. As for our lesson tonight, we mustn't concentrate solely on this young woman, who committed suicide under such dramatic conditions. In every neighborhood, there are men and women with great responsibilities, but who display disastrous and destructive passions in the area of the sentiments, in business and in social relationships. There are minds unbalanced by imprudence in nearly every part of this world. We have been careless about the smallest of things. The ocean is large; the drop of water is tiny, but the ocean is nothing more than a mass of drops gathered together. Using divine symbolism, our Master tells us about the mustard seed. Let's remember that the field of our heart is filled with thorny weeds that have dwelled there perhaps for many centuries in a terrible wasteland, so of course we should not expect a miraculous harvest. It is essential to cultivate the soil and care for what has been planted. The mustard seed that Jesus refers to is a person's gesture, word or thought. There are many people who speak a lot about humility, but they never show a gesture of obedience. We will never experience goodness without beginning to be good. We must do some little thing before we can build great things. The Lord often taught that the kingdom of heaven is within us. Well, it is there, within ourselves, that we must develop the ultimate work of divine accomplishment, without which we will be nothing more than highly imprudent individuals. The forest also began with tiny seeds. And spiritually speaking, we have lived in the dense forest of ills created by ourselves due to our carelessness in choosing spiritual seeds. The conversation of one hour, the thought of one day, the gesture of one moment can represent a great deal in our lives. Let's be careful with the little things and select the mustard seeds of the kingdom of heaven. Let's remember that Jesus taught nothing needlessly. Every time we 'take' these mustard seeds – according to the divine word – and sow them in our inner field, we will receive all the help we need from the Lord. He will shower us with blessings, the sun of eternal love, the sublime vitality of the higher planes. Our sowing will grow, and in a short time we will achieve higher spiritual accomplishments. My children, let us learn the science of how to begin, remembering Jesus' goodness at all times. The Master does not forsake us; he lovingly follows us and inspires our hearts. Above all, let us have confidence and joy!"

I noticed that Fabio had withdrawn his hand from the widow's forehead and that she had begun to meditate like someone whose thought was fading away into the distance.

There was great emotion in the assembly invisible to the children, who, in their turn, also seemed impressed.

Dona Isabel again looked at her children maternally and said:

"Now let's talk for a bit."

36

Mother and Children

During the gospel commentary, I had made some interesting observations. Like with Ismalia when we were listening to her sublime melody, Fabio's interpretation of the Gospel was filled with spiritual wonders that transcended Dona Isabel's receptive ability. Isidoro's widow seemed to retain only part of the teaching.

Hence, the children received the lesson according to the mediumistic abilities of their mother, whereas the full teaching was transmitted to the rest of us with all of its wonderful content of beauty.

Considerate as ever, our instructor explained:

"Don't be surprised at this phenomenon! Each one receives spiritual light according to his capacity. There are many fellow spirits gathered here who have a harder time registering Fabio's commentary than do the children themselves. They are still greatly limited.

There was great respect in all the discarnates present.

Fabio Aleto sat on a higher plane, while Isidoro took his place next to his wife in the kindly impulse of a father who lovingly approaches his beloved children to converse affectionately with them.

At that instant, little Marieta, who looked to be about seven, took advantage of a moment when no one was speaking in order to ask her mother in a moving tone:

"Mama, if Jesus is so good, then why do we eat only once a day here at home? At Dona Fausta's house they have two meals: lunch and dinner. Neli told me that when Papa was still around it was also like that, but now ... why is it like this?"

The widow smiled a bit sadly and said:

"Well, Marieta, you seem to be quite concerned about this matter. We must not subject all our thoughts to the needs of the stomach. How long have we been eating our daily meal now and enjoying good health? How much benefit are we reaping from this frugality with food?"

Joaninha intervened, adding:

"Mama's right. I've seen a lot of people get sick by abusing food."

"Besides that," added Isabel, comforted, "you can be sure that Jesus blesses the bread and water of all those who are truly thankful for the divine gifts. It is true that Isidoro left before us, but we've never lacked what we need. We have our little house, our spiritual togetherness and our good friends. And you can be sure that Papa's still working for us."

All of us were touched at this point in the conversation, and Isidoro wiped his tear-dampened eyes.

Noemi, the youngest little one, said in an innocent voice:

"That's right; it's true! I saw Papa helping to hold the cake that Dona Cora brought us on Sunday."

"I did too, Noemi," said Isabel, her eyes lively and shining. "Papa continues to help us."

And turning to the others, she added:

"When we know how to love and wait, my children, we are not separated from our dear ones who've died in the physical realm. Let us be certain of Jesus' protection!..."

Marieta, seeming to be perfectly calm now, agreed:

"When you talk, Mama, I feel that it's all true! How good Jesus is! But what if we didn't have you? I've seen abandoned beggar children. Maybe they have nothing at all to eat; maybe they don't have friends like ours! Ah! How grateful to heaven we should be!..."

The widow was visibly comforted at hearing these words and exclaimed with deep emotion:

"Very good, my child! We should never complain but always praise. And perhaps you wouldn't be able to understand the situation if our table had plenty."

I observed, however, that the twelve-year-old boy was not sharing in that torrent of blessings. There was a constant exchange of luminous vibrations between Dona Isabel and her four daughters as if they were at one in the same ideal and united in a single position; however, the boy remained spiritually distant, closed within a circle of darkness. From time to time he smiled ironically, insensitive to the significance of the moment. Availing himself of the lengthy pause, he asked his mother less respectfully:

"Mama, what do you think poverty is?"

Dona Isabel answered very serenely:

"My son, I think that poverty is one of the best opportunities available for spiritual growth. I'm convinced that wealthy people have a great task to fulfill, but I believe that, besides their mission in the world, poor people are freer and happier. In poverty, it's easier to find sincere friendship, the vision of God's assistance, the treasures of nature, and the wealth of simple and pure joys. Of course I'm not referring to idle and ungrateful people. I'm referring to the poor who work and keep the faith. It's very difficult for people with great financial resources to know how to discern between affection and petty self-interest; believing they can do anything by themselves, they don't always understand divine protection. Because they have given in to the addiction to comfort, they have distanced themselves more from the blessings of nature, and because they always seek to satisfy their own whims, they restrict their capacity to be happy and to confide in the world."

Despite the profound beauty of her opinion, the boy remained indifferent and responded, somewhat upset:

"Unfortunately, I can't agree with you. Even kindergarten children believe otherwise."

Isabel changed her expression and assumed an attitude of one who instructs with a sense of responsibility and added:

"We're not in kindergarten here, my son. We are in the 'garten' of our home and it behooves us to know that, even though the blossoms are always beautiful, life cannot move forward without the blessing of the fruit. Wherever we go in the world, we will receive news involving venomous lies. We must watch our hearts, Joaozinho, and appreciate the blessings that Jesus sends us."

The boy, however, revealing enormous inner rebellion, retorted:

"Don't you think it would be more reasonable for us to rent this room so we could have some extra money? Yesterday, I was talking with Mr. Maciel on my way home from school. He would pay us well so he could have a furniture storage place here."

Dona Isabel, firm but not irritated, was direct with her answer:

"You should know, my son, that as long as we respect the memory of your father, this room will be devoted solely to our Gospel activities. I've already told you the story of our home worship service and I don't want you to be blind regarding the blessings of Christ. Later on, Joaozinho, when you set out on your own in the material struggle, you can build houses to rent if you so desire. But for now you shall have to regard this room as something sacred to your mother."

"And if I insist?" asked the arrogant boy, grumpily.

The widow, very calm, explained firmly:

"If you insist, you will be punished. I'm not a mother to create dangerous illusions in the hearts of the children God has entrusted to me. Since I love you all very much, I must point you in the right direction."

The boy wanted to retort, but it seemed to me that the light issuing from Isabel's chest area confused his rebellious spirit, and I saw him become still against his wishes, sullen and angry. I deeply admired that kind woman, who addressed her oldest daughter as a friend, her younger ones as a mother, and her proud son as a sensible and conscientious instructor.

Aniceto also seemed satisfied and said to us in a meaningful tone:

"The Gospel brings balance to the soul."

Little Neli was frightened and asked humbly:

"Mama, don't let Joaozinho rent the room!"

The widow smiled, caressed her daughter's little face and affirmed:

"Joaozinho won't do that; he knows that his mama means what she says. Let's not talk about this any more, Neli."

And looking at the clock, she addressed her eldest:

"Joaninha, my daughter, pray, giving thanks in our name. Our time is up."

The young girl, with a noble and affectionate expression, thanked the Lord, touching our hearts.

37

In the Home Sanctuary

After the family service was over, one of our fellow spirits also gave thanks.

"Let us hope that these storehouses of sentiment multiply," said Aniceto emotionally. "The world may create new industries, build new skyscrapers, erect statues and cities, but without the blessings of the home, there will never be true happiness."

"Blessed are those who cultivate peace in the home," exclaimed a kindly woman, who had been sitting with us during the meeting.

Two coworkers from Nosso Lar served us a simple, light meal, which I cannot describe here for lack of analogous terms.

"In support posts like this one," explained our friendly instructor, "it's possible to preserve the purity of our nutritional substances. In this sanctuary, the lower elements do not find an environment conducive to their proliferation. There's enough light here to neutralize any manifestation of the darkness."

And while Isidoro's human family was partaking of a sparing meal of tea and toast in a nearby sitting room, we enjoyed our light repast intermixed with uplifting and healthy conversation.

The environment continued animated and joyful.

A little after 11:00 p.m. the widow retired with the children to their modest bedroom.

The sensation of peace was impossible to describe.

Aniceto, Vicente and I went with some other friends to the small garden bordering the house.

The velvety flowers were pleasantly scented. The spiritually clear ambience chased away the shadows of the night.

Breathing the caressing breezes wafting in from Guanabara Bay, I noticed for the first time a delicate phenomenon that I had never seen before. While her mother was conversing with a friend, a sweet little girl nonchalantly picked a fragrant carnation with a cry of joy. I saw her pick the flower and pull it from the stem, whereupon the material part of the carnation wilted almost at once. The woman scolded her:

"What have you done, Regina? We have no right to disturb the order of things. Don't do it again, my daughter! You've upset Mama!"

Aniceto, smiling good-naturedly, discreetly explained:

"That is our sister Emilia, a worker in Nosso Lar, who has come to meet her still incarnate husband."

"And will he be coming here?" asked Vicente curiously.

"He will come through the doors of physical sleep," added our smiling guide. "These occurrences happen in the physical realm by the thousands every night. For most incarnate brothers and sisters, sleep entails only the physiological or emotional disturbances to which they have succumbed; however, there are a great many people who, with more or less precision, are capable of developing this sort of exchange between spirits."

I was surprised. With its vast array of general services, this interesting place to which Aniceto had brought us made me intensely happy. I could foresee new activities around every corner.

Although light surrounded us, I noticed that the skies were promising heavy showers soon. The light breezes were suddenly becoming strong winds. Nevertheless, the feelings of peace were extremely pleasant.

"The wind on the earth's surface is always a heavenly blessing," remarked Aniceto succinctly. "We can surmise its divine character because of our current state. The atmospheric pressure on incarnates is approximately 33,000 pounds."

"Nevertheless, it's interesting to notice that we don't feel that much weight on our own shoulders," added Vicente.

"It's the difference between the vehicles of manifestation," explained Aniceto politely. "That is, our bodies and those of our incarnate fellow spirits display an essential difference. Let's imagine the earth's surface as an ocean of oxygen. Terrestrial individuals are heavy elements moving along the bottom of this ocean, whereas we spirits are drops of oil that can rise to the top without too much difficulty because of the quality of the matter we are made of."

At this point in his explanation, I noticed that dark shapes – some of them monstrous – were crawling along the street, looking for suitable shelter. I was appalled to see that several were heading in our direction; however, after a few steps they withdrew, frightened. They aroused a feeling of dread. Many looked like real animals wandering the streets. I must confess that an uncontrollable fear had invaded my heart.

Calm as always, Aniceto reassured us:

"You don't have to be afraid," he said. "Whenever a storm threatens, roving beings from the darkness wander about looking for shelter. They are ignorant spirits roaming the streets, enslaved to the strongest sensations of the physical senses. They are still clinging to the lowest aspects of earthly experience, and so the showers bother them as much as they would an ordinary person who was far from home. They prefer places of nighttime entertainment, where idleness finds an escape in debauchery. When these are not available, they enter open residences since the physical plane still has the same characteristic density."

And showing interest in increasing the value of this moment's lesson, he added:

"Look how they start to head this way and then run away, frightened and disconcerted. We are reaping one more lesson regarding the effects of prayer. We will never be able to list all of its benefits. Every time someone prays in a home, there is a marked improvement in its ambience. Each prayer from the heart is an electromagnetic emission of comparative power. For this very reason, the Gospel home worship service is not just a study for inner illumination, but also an advanced means of outward defense because of the spiritual light surrounding it. Those who pray bear an impenetrable armor. The home that cultivates prayer becomes a fortress. Do you understand? The spirits of darkness experience a strong jolt when they come into contact with the luminous vibrations of this home sanctuary, and that is why they stay away and look for other paths..."

In a few moments, we reentered the blessed room of the modest residence.

As if I were crossing a wonderland full of surprises, another incident aroused my profound amazement.

Isidoro and Isabel approached us arm in arm, radiating happiness. That poor widow of this humble neighborhood was now beautifully dressed in spite of the remarkable simplicity of her presence. She was smiling happily at her husband's side; she saw us and greeted us warmly:

"My friends," she said serenely, "my husband and I are going on an instructive excursion tonight. I'm leaving our children with you for a few hours and I thank you in advance for your care and attention."

"Go, my daughter!" replied an elderly woman. "Let your body rest. Leave the children with us. Go in peace!"

The couple left with the expression of sublime commitment.

Our guide leaned toward us and said:

"Have you noticed how divine happiness expresses itself in the sleep of the righteous? I know of few incarnate souls with the good fortune of this admirable woman, who has been able to learn the science of individual sacrifice."

38

Hard at Work

We remained hard at work in Dona Isabel's cozy living room. Outside, it had begun to rain heavily, but we felt far removed from the torrential downpour.

In the early hours of dawn, the activity intensified. Many individuals were coming and going.

"In this spiritual work retreat," our guide explained, "many brothers and sisters are in a realm that incarnates would call a dream. In this line of work, it's not easy to transmit messages of an instructive nature using ordinary places, because they tend to be contaminated with less-than-worthy mental matter. In spiritually uplifting support posts, however, where we are able to accumulate larger amounts of positive energies from the higher spirit planes, we are able to offer great benefits to those who are incarnate on the planet."

I added to my own observations, noting that many of the new arrivals seemed to be unsteady convalescents; some were standing up, supported by loving arms. They were incarnate friends who were availing themselves of the partial detachment of their spirit through physical sleep, and who were joining us to take advantage of the aid of generous and dedicated spirits. I realized, however, that most of them did not understand very well what was being said to them. Many appeared unwell and uncomprehending. They smiled childishly, showing a willingness to receive our guidance but a great inability to retain it. I studied these situations with understandable wonder. Helpful as always, Aniceto helped resolve my perplexity:

"As soon as incarnating spirits undergo the consolidation of the physical ties, they become subject to the imperious laws dominating earth. Between them and us there is a thick veil: the wall of vibrations. Without the temporary obliteration of memory, they would not experience a true renewal of their opportunity as incarnates. If our realm were freely open to them, they would forget their immediate obligations and would lean toward idleness, which would jeopardize their evolution. That is why they are rarely lucid while on our side of the veil. In most cases, while they are with us they remain unsteady, weakened... Observe that young incarnate woman conversing with her grandma, who works with us in Nosso Lar."

As he said this, Aniceto pointed to a group nearby.

With shining eyes and firm gestures, the old woman was hugging her languid and very pale granddaughter.

"My grandchild," exclaimed the little old lady in a firm tone, "don't give so much importance to obstacles. Forget about those who are hounding you; don't hate anyone. Guard your spiritual peace more than anything else. Your mother cannot help you now, but she does believe that our lives continue. Grandma will not forget you. Slander, my child, is a serpent that threatens the heart; however, if we face it head on, strongly and peacefully, we will soon see that the serpent has no life of its own. It's a toy viper that breaks like glass in our hands. And once the toy is conquered, instead of a serpent, we'll have a flower of virtue. Don't be afraid, dear! Don't miss the sacred opportunity to testify to your understanding of Jesus!..."

The young woman didn't answer, but her semi-lucid eyes were filled with tears. She showed a vague acknowledgement of divine comfort, resting in the loving arms of the devoted old woman.

"Will this sister remember anything when she wakes up in her physical body?" I asked our guide, intrigued.

Aniceto smiled and explained:

"Since her grandmother is more advanced from the point of view of the planes of life on which they each dwell, the young woman is under the spiritual control of her benefactress. Therefore, there is a reciprocal magnetic current between them, but I must point out that her grandmother retains a positive ascendancy. The granddaughter doesn't see her environment accurately, nor does she hear everything that is said to her. Let's not forget that disengagement during ordinary physical sleep is partial, and that the sight and hearing that are peculiar to incarnates are also restricted. Thus, the phenomenon is more of a spiritual union than one of sensorial perceptions per se. The young woman is receiving real comfort, spirit to spirit. When she awakens behind the dense veil of matter, however, she will not remember all the details of the happy encounter we have just witnessed. She will awaken feeling encouraged and refreshed, but will be unable to identify the cause of her restored good spirits. She will say that she dreamed about her grandmother in a place where there were a lot of people, but she won't be able to recall the details, adding that in her dream she saw a threatening snake, which then turned into a glass serpent that broke in her hands, only to become a fragrant flower whose aroma she still pleasantly remembers. She will affirm that a supreme comfort flooded her soul and down deep she will understand the comforting message that was given to her."

"But won't she recall the words she heard?" asked Vicente, curious.

"She would have to have acquired profound lucidity in the realm of physical existence," continued Aniceto. "And I should explain that she will remember the symbolic images of the viper and the flower because she is in a magnetic relationship with her venerable grandma, and is thus receiving the emission of her positive thoughts. Her benefactress doesn't just speak; she also sends out thoughts with a great deal of energy. Her granddaughter, however, cannot see or hear as she normally does, but she can clearly perceive the mental creations of her elderly friend, and will talk about the symbols she glimpsed and stored in her genuine and deep memory. Hence, it will not be difficult for her to grasp the essence of what her kindly grandmother wanted to communicate to her suffering heart, informing her that slander, when it wounds a peaceful conscience, is nothing but a lying serpent that transforms itself into a flower of new virtue when confronted with the valor of serene and Christian courage."

The lesson was deeply significant. I was beginning to acquire some broad notions as to the exchange between the two spheres. I thought about the lengthy efforts of those who investigate the world of dreams. How much psychological wealth could be gained if researchers could move the focus of their study from physiological events to the realm of spiritual truths! I was reminded of psychoanalysis and the instinctive inferior manifestations dealt with in the Freudian thesis.

Perceiving my inner thoughts, our devoted mentor addressed me in particular:

"Freud was a great missionary of science; however, like any other incarnate spirit, he had certain limitations. He did a great deal, but not everything, in the area of psychological research."

From our instructor's hesitation, I perceived that he did not wish to enter into a detailed examination of that famous theory. Remembering, however, the extraordinary importance attributed by the great scientist to the lower inclinations, I asked a bit timidly:

"But are there meeting centers for spirits unbalanced in evil, just as here there are centers for those who are interested in the good?"

Our kindly mentor smiled benevolently and said:

"There can be no doubt about it. Through magnetic currents susceptible to being set in motion when incarnates are asleep, lower obsessions, ongoing persecutions, low class psychic exploitations, destructive vampirism and various temptations are maintained. There are still relatively few of our incarnate brothers and sisters who know how to sleep for the good..."

And with an expressive gesture, he concluded:

"O Lord, keep us from falling once again..."

39

Never-ending Work

At dawn I noticed that Aniceto was welcoming several more friends, with whom he was speaking privately. Our esteemed guide informed us politely that he was in charge of several tasks according to Telesforo's instructions. He was obliged to treat them in a private manner, although he would not hide their main objective from us, which was the active combat against a large group of ignorant discarnate spirits gathered together for evil purposes.

While he was engaged in private conversation, we in turn were listening to other friends involved with routine spiritual work.

The day was now dawning with magnificent splendor. We had the feeling that the night rain had swept away the darkness from the firmament.

Judging by the number of spirit workers who had stayed over night in the humble little house, I recognized the importance of that service center, so hidden from the eyes of the world.

A woman, who had approached us, exclaimed with feeling:

"May the Lord reward our sister Isabel, granting her strength to resist the temptations along the path. Because I came to rest at this loving retreat, I was able to find my poor daughter and stop her from committing suicide. Thanks be to Divine Providence!"

Unable to restrain my desire to learn, I asked curiously:

"But how did you find her, my sister?"

"In a dream," answered the kindly old lady. "My Dalva was widowed three years ago, and eleven months ago I too left her alone by discarnating. The poor thing couldn't bear her suffering as she should and she allowed herself to fall into the clutches of malevolent spirits who were plotting her ruin. I approached her during the day, but my efforts were useless. With her mind absorbed in business and material complications, she couldn't feel my influence. I needed to meet with her at night, but that was not easy because I'm not spiritually evolved enough to operate alone, and the group I serve couldn't spend an entire night on earth to help me out. It was then that a friend brought me to this Nosso Lar support post. As I rested here I was able to act with the groups involved in its ongoing work, and was helped by untiring workers for the good."

"And were you able to achieve your purpose easily?" asked Vicente, interested.

"Thanks to Jesus!" answered the woman, showing enormous satisfaction. "Now I know my daughter has received my affectionate suggestions and I'm sure she will heed my requests."

"Listen, my friend," I asked, "are there many Nosso Lar support posts like this one?"

"From what I've been told, there are quite a few of them in the corporeal realm. They represent other spirit colonies not only here but also in other cities of Brazil. In these centers, there are always advanced opportunities that are indispensable for outfitting us for the struggle."

At that moment, we were greeted by two fellow spirits, with whom we had spoken during the night and who had aroused our sincere affinity.

"What?" I asked. "Are you leaving so soon?"

"We're going to work," one of them answered me. "Tonight, there will be a Gospel study and we must help our ignorant and suffering brothers and sisters who are capable of coming here."

"Is there that sort of job too?" I asked, amazed.

"Why not, my friend? Jesus himself said centuries ago that the harvest is great. There is work for everyone. And you must realize that this Christian assistance support post has been functioning non-stop for nearly twenty years."

"But have you yourselves been here since it was first founded? I asked.

He quickly explained:

"No. There are many like us who do an internship here. Only a few of Isidoro and Isabel's workers have been stationed here since the beginning of the institution. The rest of us, however, do not work here for more than two consecutive years. A support post like this one is always an active and holy school, and those who have a spirit of goodwill should not miss the chance to learn."

"Forgive me for asking so many questions," I replied, "but I'd like to know if you are the only ones with the skills needed for recruiting those who are ignorant and suffering in order for them to be instructed and consoled."

"No. Hildegardo and I are assistants for only a few blocks in the city. There are many, many coworkers in this line of help."

Just then, one of the brothers, who seemed to be a member of the place's guidance group, approached and addressed our friend:

"Vieira, I suggest that you and Hildegardo observe our doctrinal criterion more carefully. It would be useless to bring vagrant or untrustworthy spirits to this place simply because you feel personally sympathetic toward them. We cannot waste time on sneering and lazy spirits, nor on those who approach our place with certain intentions of a lower nature. There will be no lack of Jesus' provisions for these people elsewhere. Remember that.

"It's not a lack of charity; it's an understanding of duty. We have a very serious work to do in the evangelization and aid program, and we cannot misuse what has been granted by our superiors of Higher Spirituality. Those who accept a commitment are held responsible for it. No matter how much you love some lazy or sarcastic spirit, don't give it any leeway. Help it privately when you have the time and opportunity, but don't drag the group into its problems. Don't forget that there are certain task centers for those who are intentionally deaf and blind."

Vieira and his colleague became very pale and didn't say a word.

When their calm and alert guide left, Vieira explained, disappointedly:

"We've been justly admonished."

And because he saw that we were eager to learn, he respectfully continued:

"Unfortunately, Hildegardo and I have some discarnate relatives in distressing spiritual situations. We brought my uncle Hilario and cousin Carlos to the last meeting, even though we knew that because of their disrespect for the divine laws in the inferior environment in which they live, neither of them was prepared for serious reflection. However, they both seemed so eager for renewal that we listened to personal sympathy, forgetting the need for proper preparation. They came with us and sat among the many listeners. But in the middle of the Gospel study they tried to take over Sister Isabel's mediumistic faculties in order to transmit a message of less uplifting content. Sensing our vigilance and surprised by the coworkers of this sanctified post, they rebelled and created a great disturbance. If it hadn't been for the magnetic barriers of the guard service, they would have caused very serious harm. The meeting was thus less fruitful because of the great waste of time. Well, naturally we were held responsible..."

"My God!" exclaimed Vicente, amazed, "what a new lesson!"

"Ah, yes, my friend," replied Vieira, resigned. "Here we must not misuse love like we do in the corporeal realm! No one is forbidden to help, to want the good, to intercede; we can all assist those we love with the resources that are appropriate, but the word 'duty' has a positive meaning here for those who wish to walk sincerely toward God."

40

Heading to the Countryside

Almost all the spirit workers were leaving the house on their way to their assorted tasks. Only a few friends involved with missions of aid and vigilance remained at Dona Isabel's residence.

I noticed that Aniceto continued to give out various instructions, confidentially addressing certain coworkers regarding the mission that Telesforo had entrusted to him.

Just before noon, however, he invited us to accompany him.

"In this support post," he said kindly, "we can find vital renewal of our strength for our work. We receive reinforcements of energy, and this provides us with the nourishment needed to continue our efforts, but we must admit that, for many of us, last night was a series of long, exhausting activities. We need some rest. We'll return at dusk."

Where were we going? I didn't know. I remembered that, even though some had actually rested in the home sanctuary during the night, most had worked intensely, and I concluded that if in the morning many had headed for their duties, others had sought needed repose.

"Where are you headed?" asked a spirit security guard who had become our friend.

Before we could answer, Aniceto explained:

"To the countryside."

And directing himself especially to Vicente and me, he remarked:

"Let's use volitation, since we have no immediate plans in the center of the city."

I noticed that I was now exercising my faculties of volitation with growing ease. The educational excursion with the stop at the Campo da Paz Rescue Outpost had done me much good. My training had improved. I felt strong enough to face vibrations of a lower order, and I mobilized my own resources without difficulty. I also noticed that my visual abilities were growing appreciably. Up to that point, I had not previously noticed what I was now very surprised to observe while volitating. Before, I had seen only people, animals, vehicles and buildings anchored to the ground. Now, my seeing abilities were expanding. From the distance, I understood the considerable weight of the air that was clinging to the surface. I had the impression that we were swimming in the upper zone of a sea of oxygen as I saw down below in roiled waters a huge number of brothers and sisters dragging themselves along heavily, burdened with heavy diving gear on the muddy ocean bed.

"Do you see those dark stains on the public street?" asked our guide, noticing our amazement and our increasing desire to learn.

Since we didn't know what they were exactly, he continued to explain:

"Those are clouds of various bacteria. They almost always float around in compact groups in obedience to the principle of affinity. Notice those arabesques of shadow..."

And he pointed out certain buildings and areas of the city.

"Notice the large grayish or completely dark areas!... Those are zones of inferior mental matter, matter that is continually exhaled by a certain class of people. If we were to take more time with our investigation, we would also see monsters that drag themselves along behind certain people, attracted by them..."

Giving a serious tone to his words, he observed:

"Humans are attacked not only by the cloud of bacteria, which is destructive to physical life, but by the perverse forms of the darkness, which threaten their mental balance. As you can see, the 'watch and pray' of the Gospel has profound importance in every situation at any time. Only people with positive mentalities in the realm of higher spirituality manage to overcome the multiple influences of a less worthy nature."

Interested in a broader explanation, however, I asked:

"But does the mental matter emitted by less evolved people have a life of its own like the nuclei of microscopic corpuscles from which bodily illnesses spring?"

Our kind mentor smiled curiously and added:

"Why not? By now, you are not unaware of the fact that people live in a psychophysical body. We cannot consider just the physiological situation per se in the realm of diseases, but we must also consider the psychic condition of the incarnate personality. You see, just as there is a cloud of bacteria produced by a sick body, there is a cloud of mental larvae produced by a sick mind in the same circumstances. So in the realm of individuals who are unaware of spiritual resources, bodies as well as souls become ill. For this very reason, in the future the medicine of the soul will absorb the medicine of the body. Currently, on earth we can provide treatment for the fleshly organism. Such a task makes the mission of comfort, instruction and relief a worthy one, but as far as real healing is concerned, we must realize that this belongs exclusively to the spirit itself."

"My God!" exclaimed Vicente, startled. "What dangers the ordinary human has to face!"

"This is why," replied Aniceto mindfully, "terrestrial existence is a glorious opportunity for those who are interested in knowledge and self-elevation. And for this same reason we teach the need for religious faith among human beings. In developing this campaign, we do not plan to intensify the disastrous passions of sectarianism, but to create a positive state of trust, optimism and healthy vitality in the mind of each incarnate fellow spirit. Until now, only faith has been able to provide this realization. Sciences and philosophies have paved the way; nonetheless, the faith that conquers death is the vital seed. Possessing its eternal value, humans find enough spiritual dynamism to fight until they have achieved a full victory over themselves."

Understanding that he needed to finish his explanation, he stated after a longer pause:

"We all need to know how to emit vibrations and how to receive them. To reach a position of balance in this situation, incarnate men and women, as well as we ourselves, are engaged in a constant struggle. And since we already know something about eternity, we must not forget that every fall jeopardizes achievement, and every noble effort invariably helps."

These explanations could not have been clearer. However, I was disconcerted by that vision of streets filled with sluggishly moving dark spots, affecting both humans and machines on the public streets.

Thirsty for knowledge, I returned to the subject:

"This lesson has incalculable value for me. And when I think of the high reproductive power of microbial flora..."

Aniceto, however, did not let me finish. Knowing beforehand my natural question, he interrupted me, exclaiming:

"Yes, Andre, had it not been for the much greater power of the sun's light, coupled with earth's magnetism – a power which intensely destroys in order to select life's manifestations on the earth's surface – microbial flora of a lower order would not have allowed the existence of a single person on the face of the earth. That is why the soil and plants are filled with curative and transforming principles."

And nodding his head expressively, he concluded:

"In spite of the immense power of this divine resource, as long as humans - the heirs of God - cultivate the lower realms of life, there will also be lower creations in sufficient number for the truceless battle that the authentic values of evolution must win."

41

Among the Trees

After a few minutes had passed, we arrived at a small rural property populated by a welcoming grove of trees.

There were orange trees in blossom as far as the eye could see. Banana plants were spread out like fans, while from afar the guava grove looked like robust patches of greenery. The soft grass invited rest. And a calm breeze was blowing lightly, whispering something through the leaves.

Aniceto gulped in long, deep breaths and said:

"Although they don't get tired like incarnates, discarnates cannot go without a rest break. In general, our operations at night are hectic and laborious. Only a third of our fellow spirits involved in service on earth remain active during the day."

And noticing our curiosity, he added:

"Moreover, it's only reasonable that it be that way. The terrestrial day belongs more appropriately to the work of incarnate spirits. People have to learn to act, bearing witness to their understanding of the divine laws. At least during a certain number of hours, they should be left more alone with their own experiences."

Our instructor friend smiled and observed:

"For humans day and night comprise a page from the book of life. Most of the time, people write their daily page alone with the ink of their own sentiments in words, thoughts, intentions and actions, and then in the 'overleaf', that is, in nighttime reflection, we help them to correct and adjust their experiences as the Lord allows it."

Our guide fell silent and we focused our attention exclusively on the beauty surrounding us. That friendly and welcoming countryside was characterized by a highly diverse environment. There were no more heavy emanations from the big city, but a light breeze scented with the most pleasant fragrances. I was reflecting on the goodness of the Lord, who had provided us with new resources, when Aniceto spoke again:

"Nature is never the same in any two places. There are no two spots on earth with climates exactly alike. Each hill, each valley has different climatic characteristics. We must realize, though, that, under any circumstance among incarnates, the countryside is a most abundant and vigorous reservoir of vital principles.

In general, all of us spirit workers appreciate the morning air when the atmosphere is also at rest and devoid of dust balls that have been converted into microscopic balloons of bacteria and other lower life-forms. However, today's work has not enabled us to rest any sooner..."

We leaned back into the velvety grass, and perceiving our thirst for knowledge, Aniceto continued:

"What I mean is that in the forest the emanations are very dense because that environment is rather impenetrable to the wind. There, the air usually becomes a suffocating element because of the excess of emissions from the lower kingdoms of nature. Likewise, in the city the atmosphere is compact and the air is also suffocating because of the mentally dense emanations of the lower groups of humans. That is why in the country we have the ideal center..."

Joyfully pointing to the swaying foliage, he added:

"Here the relatively balanced peace of nature reigns. There is neither the wildness of the virgin forest nor the suffocation of human fluids. The countryside is our bounteous main path, our earthly harmony, our desirable rest."

Cuddled by the song of a few solitary doves, we rested for a few hours, sheltered delightfully in nature's temple.

With the first colors of twilight, Aniceto invited us for a quick walk around the vicinity.

I realized that we were feeling much more full of life.

Only after we had walked around for a few minutes did I notice that there were a great number of spirit workers in the neighboring areas.

Perceiving my questions, our mentor kindly explained:

"The countryside is also a vast workshop for our effective work together."

And pointing to the workers, who were coming and going, he commented:

"The vegetable kingdom has many, many coworkers. It is possible that you don't know that many brothers and sisters are preparing themselves to deserve a new incarnation in the world by offering their services to the lower kingdoms. Work with the Lord is a living school wherever we may be."

At that moment our attention was attracted by a great deal of commotion on the nearby road.

We headed in that direction, following Aniceto, who seemed to have guessed what was going on.

I then observed an interesting scene: a man was lying on the ground in a pool of blood next to a small cart pulled by a mule that was showing signs of great agitation. Two incarnates were hastily providing first aid to the wounded man. "We have to get him to the farm without wasting time," said one of them, distressed. "I'm afraid his skull is fractured." The number of discarnates helping the small group was very large, however.

A spirit friend who looked like the leader of the group welcomed us with respect and kindness, and explained what had happened. The wagoneer had been kicked by the mule and they had to rescue the wounded man.

When the situation calmed down, this hierarchical superior called to a road guard and asked him:

"Glicerio, how could you let something like this happen? This section of the road is under your direct responsibility."

The subordinate replied respectfully:

"I did everything I could to save this man, who, by the way, has a wife and kids. My efforts were fruitless because of his recklessness. For a long time I have been trying to surround him with care whenever he passed this way; however, the wretch doesn't have the least respect for the natural gifts of God. He is unspeakably rough on the animals that help him earn his pay. All he knows how to do is to shout at them, get angry, beat and hurt them. His mind is closed to suggestions of gratitude. He respects only profanity and the whip. Today, he harassed and punished the poor mule that helps him so much that he looked more like an animal himself ... When he nearly went out of his mind because of so much fury and ingratitude, my help as a spirit was no longer effective. Tormented by his driver's outbursts of anger, the humble mule attacked him with his hoof. What else could I have done? I fulfilled my duty..."

His superior, who had been listening attentively to his allegations, replied without hesitation:

"You are right."

And since he was looking to Aniceto for approval, our guide affirmed:

"Let's help this man as much as we can and fulfill our duty to the good, but let's not disdain the lesson here. This imprudent worker has punished himself. Anger is punished by its consequences. Evil follows evil. If animals – our brothers and sisters in the great home of life – provide us with the worth of their service, we, in turn, should give them the worth of education. Now, no one can educate if they hate, nor can they build anything useful with fury and brutality."

And pointing to the group that was taking the wounded man to a nearby house, he calmly concluded:

"As an ordinary man, our poor friend will suffer for many days, confined to his bed; amidst the afflictions of his family members, it will take him quite awhile to reestablish his organic balance. As an eternal spirit, however, he has received a useful and needed lesson."

Greatly surprised, I observed our guide's serenity and I began to understand that no one disrespects nature without the painful blow of retribution.

42

The Word in a Rural Setting

Now that the explanations about the unpleasant incident had ended, the hierarchical superior of that large team of spirit workers asked our guide politely:

"Noble Aniceto, we would like to make the most of your presence. Would you mind giving us a scripture lesson now that the day is about over?"

Aniceto readily agreed.

I noticed that everyone was very much interested.

I was greatly surprised to see the farm workers bring our esteemed mentor a book, which I had no trouble identifying: it was a copy of the New Testament. Aniceto opened it confidently as if he knew exactly where to find the appropriate passage.

He gazed at the page he had chosen and began to meditate. A sublime light began to halo his head. There was profound silence as all the coworkers showed great anticipation for what Aniceto would say to them. Everything in nature seemed majestic and peaceful. A herd of cattle had approached us, attracted by magnetic energies beyond my understanding. Even a few humble mules had arrived from afar, and the birds had settled down in the dense foliage without making a peep. The only sound to be heard was the light, soft voice of the wind whispering harmony and freshness. Dressed in the liquid gold of the sunset, the landscape could not have been more beautiful. Except for the natural rusticity of our colorful surroundings, the setting brought back fond memories of the green halls of Nosso Lar.

Aniceto, gazing intently at a passage in the sacred book, read aloud Romans 8:19-21:

"For the creation earnestly waits in expectation for the manifestation of the children of God. For the creature became subject to futility (not willingly, but because of him who subjected it) in the hopes that the creation itself shall also be delivered from the bondage of corruption and brought into the glorious liberty of the children of God."

He then reflected for a few instants and remarked with noticeable inspiration:

"Brothers and sisters, let us receive the blessing of the countryside, praising the love and wisdom of our

Father! Let us extol the supreme Spirit of Life, which breathes into us the eternal power of unending renewal! Let us ponder these words of the Apostle to the Gentiles in order to discern their divine content!... Nature has been waiting for millennia for humans to begin to comprehend. It has not been nourished with hope alone, however; it has been living in ardent expectation, waiting for the understanding and help of spirits incarnating on earth, that is, the children of God. Meanwhile, the forces of nature continue suffering the oppression of human vanity. However, my friends, this occurs because the Lord also holds out hope for the deliverance of beings enslaved on earth so that freedom in the glory of men and women may also occur. I know your sacrifices intimately, you selfless spirit workers on earthly soil! As is the case in many other areas of the planet, many of you have remained here in order to help your incarnate fellow spirits, who are chained to the illusion of material gain. How many times has your help been converted into exploitation in the realm of earthly matters? Most of earth's caretakers demand everything but offer nothing in return. While you carefully oversee the maintenance of the fundamentals of life, you have seen civilization acting like a powerful threshing machine. You have seen men and women – our brothers and sisters – turning themselves into little Molochs of bread, meat and wine, completely immersed in vices of the sentiments and excesses of food, unconcerned about their huge debt to nature, so loving and generous. They oppress the creatures of the lower kingdoms, harm the beneficial energies of life, show ingratitude for the sources of the good, and mind their rural industries more out of vanity and ambition for gain than out of the spirit of love and usefulness. They are also nothing more than the unfortunate servants of harried passions. They draw up deceitful plans to gain riches that lead them to their ruin; they write treatises on economic policies that result in destructive wars; they develop commerce for unfair gain, reaping international turmoil leading to poverty; they dominate the weak and exploit them, but they themselves awaken soon afterward amongst monsters of hatred! It is to them, our incarnate friends, that we must turn our attention with a spirit of tolerance and fraternity. Let us continue to help them now and forever! Let us not forget that the Lord holds out hope for their future! Let us listen to the cries of creation as it pleads for the light of human reason, but also, let us not forget the tears of these slaves to corruption – among whose ranks we ourselves were members until yesterday – helping them to awaken to divine consciousness for eternal life! Even though they are encircled by their vanity and insolence, we will continue to help them, nonetheless. The Lord grants an increase in evolutionary progress to self-sacrificing souls. He will not forget the useful tree, the exterminated animal, the humble being that is consumed for the benefit of another! As for us, let us work to awaken our brothers and sisters concerning our debt to Mother Nature. Whenever we return to reincarnate, surrounding ourselves in the fluids of the physical realm, we always exaggerate our intake of nitrogen. We convert into a worldwide tragedy what might otherwise comprise a serene and edifying pursuit. As we know, no organism on earth can live without nitrogen, and although humans move within an ocean of it, inhaling an average of a thousand liters per day, they – like all other living beings on the planet – cannot assimilate the nitrogen in the air. Unlike ordinary oxygen, for the time being, the Lord does not allow for the creation of cells in the living organisms of our world that have the ability to spontaneously absorb this extremely important life-sustaining element. Only plants, those untiring workers of the planet, can draw it from the soil, thereby securing it to enhance the lives of other beings. Each grain of wheat is a nitrogenated blessing for sustaining living beings; each piece of fruit from the earth is a container of sugar and albumen, full of the nitrogen indispensable to the organic balance of living beings. In essence, all the farming and ranching industries represent nothing more than the organized and methodical pursuit of this precious element of life. If humans could utilize approximately ten grams of the thousand liters of nitrogen they breathe daily, the earth would be transformed into a truly spiritual paradise. But if the Lord has given us much, it is reasonable for him to demand the collaboration of our own efforts in constructing our happiness. Even in Nosso Lar we are still far from the great ability to nourish ourselves spontaneously and completely with atmospheric energies. Moreover, my friends, humans have transformed the quest for nitrogen into an activity of frenzied passion, hurting and being hurt, offending and being offended, enslaving and becoming slaves, segregated in dense darkness! Let us help them to understand in order to implement a new age. Let us help them to love the earth instead of wantonly exploiting it, and to value the work of animals without destroying them! When that finally comes to pass, the slaughterhouse will be converted into a place of cooperation, where people will help lower beings and where these in turn will meet the needs of humans, and trees will live amidst the respect that is due them. In that sublime era, industry will glorify the good. Perceiving our understanding, goodwill and veneration for the divine laws, the Lord will - at least in part - offer us a solution to the technical problem of securing the atmosphere's nitrogen. Let us teach our brothers and sisters that life is not to be comprised of incessant robbery, where plants are made to damage the soil, where animals exterminate plants and where people murder animals. Rather, life is an activity of divine sharing and generous cooperation, and we will not disrupt it without causing serious damage to our own position as responsible and evolved creatures! Let us not condemn! Let us always be of help!"

The group, as well as ourselves, was deeply impressed.

Aniceto fell silent and sympathetically watched the nearby animals and birds as if he were sending deep thoughts of love to them, and then he closed the holy book with these words:

"We notice in Paul's letter that the creation anxiously awaits the cooperation of the incarnate children of God! We agree that the creatures of the lower kingdoms have borne the weight of great iniquities! Let us continue to help them, but let us not get lost in vain contentions. Humans are also waiting for our spiritual manifestation! In this way, let us help everyone in the chapter of great understanding."

43

Before the Meeting

Spiritual preparations for the meeting were busy and complex.

We returned to Dona Isabel's residence a little before 6 p.m. and the room was already filled with busy workers.

Finding some of the activities unusual, I asked our guide a few questions, which he kindly answered:

"Carrying out an effective spiritual work session is not such a simple thing. Whenever there are incarnate fellow spirits devotedly and cheerfully involved in their labor, with no worries, unhealthy experiences or unreasonable apprehensions, we can set vast resources in motion to achieve success. Of course, we cannot take part in childish activities in this respect. Those who don't wish to perform their obligations with due seriousness will surely encounter less serious spirits, because physical death does not mean automatic renewal for those who have not endeavored to renew themselves. Wherever frivolous souls are gathered, there frivolousness will be. In Isabel's case, however, we are always ready and willing to help her spiritually constructive efforts. In all areas of evolution, it's natural that the sincere and effective worker should receive increasingly ample resources. Wherever activity for the good is found, a higher order of spiritual cooperation will remain there."

Our kindly friend fell silent.

I continued to observe the laborious activities of some of the brothers and sisters as they were dividing the room in an unusual way by utilizing long fluidic bands of some sort. Aniceto came to the rescue of my perplexity, explaining thoughtfully:

"These friends are performing the work of setting up safeguards around the area. A few dozen sufferers will be brought in for tonight's work, and it is essential to limit the area of their influence in this family temple. That is why our fellow spirits are preparing the necessary magnetic divisions."

I was impressed at noticing that they were magnetizing the air itself.

However, our instructor kindly informed me:

"Don't be too impressed, Andre. In our line of work, magnetism is the predominant force and we are compelled to make widespread use of it."

And he concluded, smiling:

"Even the priests of ancient Egypt were aware of the fact that to achieve certain effects it was essential to impregnate the atmosphere with spiritual elements, saturating it with the positive forces of their will. To disseminate the light of the Gospel to discarnates, varied and complex provisions are necessary, without which everything would merely result in more disturbances. This center is tiny if considered from the material point of view, but it has great meaning for us. We must be vigilant; let's not forget that."

While the spiritual preparation continued at full steam, Dona Isabel and Joaninha in turn were taking care of various arrangements for the meeting. They went over the entire area with brooms and feather dusters. They then covered the table with a snow-white tablecloth and brought in small vessels of pure water.

At an order from one of the superiors of the church-home, the guards spread out around the simple dwelling. The noteworthy supervision of the benefactors was apparent in the smallest details. Everything displayed order, service and simplicity.

A few minutes after 6:00, the needy began to arrive from a sphere invisible to the ordinary human.

If any average people were granted a glimpse – however slight – of this group of disturbed and suffering discarnate spirits, they would undoubtedly change their attitudes in their everyday lives. In this respect, we should likewise include the majority of Spiritists, who regularly attend instructional meetings but who show no motivation for self-education; they have a vague idea of the spirit world but continue to be concerned with minding their habitual selfishness. The panorama of individual rectification after physical death is so extensive and varied that I lack the words to explain my immense surprise.

Those skeletal faces aroused everyone's compassion. Disturbed spirits were coming into the room in small groups, accompanied by their fraternal guides. They looked like corpses arisen from their deathbeds. Some of them moved with great difficulty. We were looking at an authentic gathering of the "lame and maimed", according to Gospel symbolism.

"Most of them," explained Aniceto, "are discouraged and embittered brothers and sisters, who want renewal without knowing how to begin the task. Here we can observe sufferers only of that sort because Isidoro and Isabel's family sanctuary is not equipped to receive intentionally wicked spirits. Each center has its own special purpose."

Indeed, the recent arrivals had deep anguish imprinted on their faces. There was a large number of sobbing women. It was truly a disturbing scene. A few spirits held their hands to their bellies or were pressing down on wounded areas. Many were wearing bandages and dressings.

"A lot of them," said Aniceto, "have yet to face the realities of corporal death. And by and large, they are all slaves to the idea of illness. There are people – and you, as doctors, have known many – who actually take pleasure in cultivating illness. They enjoy detailed diagnoses, monitor with indescribable passion the appearance of signs of death in their bodies, and study theories regarding their illnesses very carefully but without taking such care in analyzing their daily obligations. And when they can't find what they're looking for in books, they count on lengthy attention from their doctors, the scrupulous care of nurses and long lectures on their illnesses, to which they are willing prisoners. After discarnating, it is far more difficult for them to understand the truth, since they continue with their dominant ideas. Sometimes, deep down, they are good souls who are dedicated to their kin and are useful in the restricted area of understanding where they have taken refuge, but nevertheless, they have been bogged down in mental contamination for many centuries."

And with a different expression, he reflected:

"It takes all of us ages to break out of the old shell of individualism. The vision of universality carries a high price tag and we aren't always willing to pay it. We don't want to renounce our old tastes and we run from making praiseworthy sacrifices. Under such circumstances, the world that prevails for a long time for the discarnate soul is the personal kingdom of our lower creations; thus, those who have cultivated illness have submitted themselves to this empire. While incarnate, it is only logical that we offer every assistance to our physical body, which functions as a sacred vessel, but fixing one's health while at the same time contaminating one's mind are two essentially contradictory approaches."

His talk was wonderfully educational; however, the growing numbers of needy spirits were calling for our help. Many were weeping quietly; others were moaning more loudly.

After a long pause, Aniceto announced:

"Let's get to work. For us spirit workers, our labor has already begun. The prayer and efforts of our incarnate fellow spirits represent the boundary for this meeting of assistance and illumination in Jesus Christ."

44

Assistance

The picture of suffering unfolding before our eyes reminded me of the environment of the Chambers of Rectification.

Aniceto joined Isidoro and said resolutely:

"Let's get to work! Let's apply some energizing passes!"

"But," I objected, "am I ready for this kind of work?"

"Why not?" asked my instructor in a firm voice. "Every skill and specialty in the world involving service sectors consists in developing our goodwill. A sincere desire to cooperate and a notion of the responsibility involved are enough for us to begin any new task successfully."

Such affirmations were encouraging.

I remembered Narcisa, dedicated sister of the unfortunate, who remained in Nosso Lar, almost never resting, like a prisoner of sacrifice. It seemed as though I could still hear her sisterly and affectionate voice: "Andre, my friend, as far as possible, never neglect helping those who suffer. As you stand at the feet of your patients, don't forget that the best medicine is the renewal of hope; if you encounter the failed and hopeless, speak to them of the divine opportunity of the future; if someday you are hounded by devious and criminal spirits, don't offer them words of cursing. Encourage, edify, educate, and awaken, without harming those who still sleep. God does wonders through deeds of goodwill!" With no further hesitation, I got down to work.

Aniceto assigned a group of six spirit patients to me, stressing:

"Apply your resources, Andre. With our collaboration, the friends who work in this house will be able to attend to other more pressing responsibilities."

The most insignificant workers for the good rejoice at the opportunity of helping out in ordinary struggles; they build themselves up in the Lord Jesus because not one of their deeds gets lost in time and space. At the moment, I was being called upon to offer real aid. I did not resort to any of my scientific methods or rely only on the techniques of official medicine, with which I had been associated in the world; instead, I remembered the humble and simple Narcisa in the Chambers of Rectification, a devoted and caring nurse who achieved much more with love than with medication.

I approached a deeply disheartened woman, remembering the example of my generous friend in Nosso Lar and knowing that I should help not just by using resolution and energy, but also tenderness and understanding.

"My sister," I said, trying to gain her trust, "let's begin with some energizing passes."

"Oh! Oh!" answered the woman. "I can't see anything; I can't see anything! Oh, the trachoma! What a wretch I am! And they talk to me about death, about a different life ... How can I get my sight back?! I want to see; I want to see!..."

"Just compose yourself," I replied, feeling encouraged. "Don't you trust in the power of Jesus? He is still healing the blind, lighting our pathway, guiding our steps!"

Only later on did I remember that, at that moment, I had forgotten all about my unwholesome curiosity. I didn't think about the impression that the trachoma had left on that spirit organism, nor was I concerned about the proper scientific expression of the phenomenon. All I saw in front of me was a suffering and needy sister. And as I became more and more willing to practice fraternal love, a different clarity began to illuminate and warm my face.

Remembering the divine influence of Jesus, I began the relieving passes over the poor woman's eyes, noticing that an enormous layer of darkness was weighing on her face. Saying encouraging words, to which I lent the best essence of my intentions, I concentrated my magnetic aid abilities on that disturbed area. Within a few seconds, the discarnate let out a shout of astonishment.

"I can see! I can see!" she exclaimed, between fear and joy. "God is great! God is great!"

And kneeling in an instinctive display of thanks, she spoke to me, deeply moved:

"Who are you, emissary of good?"

I was overcome by a profound emotion that I could not suppress. The goodness of the Eternal confounded me. Who was I to heal anyone? But the joy of that spirit, freed from darkness, affirmed an event that I did not want to believe. The light of that gift revealed more strongly the dark depths of my own imperfections; the tears rolled down my cheeks, and I was unable to hold them back in the hidden recesses of my heart. While the spirit patient broke down in tears of praise, I was also absorbed in a wave of new thoughts. The incident had surprised me. I wanted to help the next patient; nevertheless, I was caught up in an odd inner fascination. Aniceto, however, approached me politely and said in a low voice:

"Andre, excessive contemplation of results can jeopardize the worker. On occasions like this, vanity usually awakens within us, making us forget the Lord. Don't forget that all good comes from him; he is the light of our hearts. We are his instruments in the tasks of love. The faithful servant is not the one who is startled at the results, nor the one who gets wrapped up in contemplating them, but the one who fulfills the divine will of the Lord and moves on."

Those words couldn't have been more meaningful. Our kindly mentor returned to the work in which he was involved, along with other brothers and sisters, and in appreciation for his loving advice I turned to the grateful woman and emphasized:

"My friend, thank Jesus and not me; I am merely an obscure servant. Furthermore, don't be too impressed with being able to see outward things; turn your visual power inward so that you can consecrate the sublime gift of sight to the Lord of Life."

I noticed that my listener was taken aback by my words, which perhaps seemed to her inopportune and transcendental, but firm again in the understanding of my duty, I approached the next patient. He was an unfortunate brother who had died in Gamboa, a victim of cancer. His entire facial area looked horrible. I applied energizing passes while ministering encouraging thoughts and words, and I noticed that the poor man began to feel considerably better. I promised I would help him check into some spirit home for treatment, recommending that he prepare his mental life to receive such a favorable benefit when the appropriate time came. Then I attended two ex-tuberculosis patients from Encantado, and afterward a woman who had discarnated in Piedade as a result of a malignant tumor, and a young man from Olaria, who had passed away from shock during surgery. None of these last four, however, showed any signs of relief. Their organic ailments and the accompanying psychic phenomena of suffering persisted.

When I had finished my allotted task, I joined my instructor and Vicente, who were waiting for me in a corner of the room.

"The activities of assistance," Aniceto explained solicitously, "proceed as you have observed here. Some feel that they are healed, while others say they've at least improved, but most seem to continue unreceptive to the aid they have received. What should interest us, however, is the sowing of the good. The germination, growth, blossom and fruit belong to the Lord."

Vicente seemed deeply impressed and remarked:

"The number of disturbed spirits is frightening. All the way from Nosso Lar to the earth, we have seen them at varying degrees of imbalance."

Aniceto smiled and said in a serious tone:

"We owe the overwhelming percentage of such afflictions to the lack of proper religious education. I am not, however, referring to the kind that comes from a priest or the mouth of one person to the ears of another. I am referring to the inner and profound religious education that people systematically deny themselves."

45

The Infirm Mind

Always watching and working, Aniceto remarked:

"Not only ill discarnates come here; notice the incarnate ones as well. Between our circle and the group of embodied brothers and sisters, the percentage of workers in relation to the number of the sick and needy is about the same."

Pointing to a well-dressed and elegant gentleman, who was conversing with Mr. Bentes, the instructor for that group, he added:

"Look at that friend, surrounded in darkness, conversing with our sister Isabel's companion. Listen to his words and then judge for yourselves."

Indeed, the gentleman he pointed out was surrounded by small clouds, mainly around his head.

Focusing my attention on him, I could hear him distinctly:

"For a long time," he affirmed emphatically, "I have been going to Spiritist meetings looking for something that would satisfy me; however," and he smiled ironically, "either I am unhappier than others or we're dealing with a worldwide deception."

Noticing his incarnate guide's respectful attitude, he continued proudly:

"I have studied a great deal and have not disregarded the sieve of strict reason. I have devoured extensive literature about human survival after death, but I still have never obtained any proof of it. Spiritism is full of alluring theses, but the subject still raises many questions. Kardec's work undeniably shows extraordinary philosophical insight, but we also find a great many new perspectives in Richet. Metapsychics has corrected many flights of imagination and has offered for public analysis more profound observations about the unknown powers of humankind. In examining these scientific truths, the dimensions of mediunism have been reduced. We need a movement of rationalization, adjusting the phenomena to appropriate criteria. Nevertheless, my dear Bentes, we live in an arena of subtle mystification, far removed from precise demonstration."

At this point, Bentes, very calm and secure in his faith, interrupted:

"I agree, Dr. Fidelis, that Spiritism should not try to avoid any kind of honest speculation; however, I believe that the Doctrine is a collection of sublime truths, which are directed primarily to the human heart. It is impossible to examine their divine grandeur with our imperfect faculties of observation or to gather their pure waters with the soiled vessel of our mind, which has been contaminated by the errors of many millennia. Furthermore, we have learned that the revelation of divine order is not the mechanical workings of the law of least effort. Let's remember that the Gospel's mission with the Master was preceded by many centuries of human effort. Before Christians died in the Roman arenas of martyrdom, how many of Jesus' precursors were sacrificed? First, we must build the receptacle; then we will receive the blessing. The Bible, the sacred book of Christians, is an encounter with human experience, filled with sweat and tears – intimately portrayed in the Old Testament – with the heavenly, sublime and pure response in the Gospel of our Lord."

The gentleman, who answered to the name of Dr. Fidelis, smiled vaguely, revealing something between irony and offended vanity.

Bentes, however, didn't miss the opportunity and continued:

"If all the serious work of human life is something sacred in our sight, then what about the expression of the divine in planetary work? And regarding the essentiality of labor in organizing the world, what would become of us if a handful of spirit friends and scholars suddenly transported us to a broad vision of more highly evolved orbs, pushing us toward them simply because of their holy esteem for us as individuals? Would we be prepared for the radical change? Would we know what life on a higher orb would be like? Will we have worked enough to understand the divine designs? And what about the earth? And our millenary debt to the planet that has borne our imperfections? How can we dwell in the higher realms without draining the swamps that lie below? These considerations become crucial for examining an argument such as yours, because we cannot accurately judge the abundant currents of a voluminous river if we see only the drops collected in the thimble of our limitations."

The obstinate scholar looked even more ironic and retorted:

"You speak as a man of faith, forgetting that my efforts are directed toward reason and science. I wish to refer to the inevitable inferences of free research, to the mediumistic farces down through time. You are aware that many scientists have examined the frauds involving mediumship in Europe and America. Well, what can you expect of a doctrine entrusted to continental deceivers?"

Bentes replied, very serenely and thoughtfully:

"You are mistaken, my friend. We would be committing a grave error if we placed all doctrinal responsibility on mediums. Mediums are simple coworkers in the work of spiritualization. They all will have to answer for what they have done with the abilities they received, just as we ourselves will be compelled to settle our accounts some day. We mustn't commit the absurdity of attributing the concentration of all divine truths to the minds of only certain individuals who are candidates for new sects of worship. The doctrine, Dr. Fidelis, is a sublime and pure fountain, inaccessible to the individualistic cravings of any one of us, a fountain from which all individuals must drink the water of their own renewal. As for the mediumistic frauds you mentioned, you must realize that so-called scientific certainty has sought to convert the noblest mediums into nervous wrecks or simple laboratory guinea pigs. Researchers, currently baptized as metapsychics, are strange tillers who swarm around the fields of service without producing anything fundamentally useful. They bend over the ground, count the grains of sand and invasive worms, determine the degree of heat and study the longitude; they observe climatic tendencies and note atmospheric variations, but to the great surprise of sincere workers, they disregard the seed."

Dr. Fidelis stopped smiling and commented:

"We shall see, we shall see ... I am waiting for a message from my loved ones to provide me with an unmistakable sign of survival after death..."

Aniceto touched us lightly and said:

"Have you noticed how this man displays a contaminated mind? He is one of those curious, ill incarnates. He has a broad education, but nevertheless, since his sentiments have been poisoned, everything that comes into his mind partakes of this general toxicity. He is a superficial researcher, as are many people. He expects everything from others; he examines his fellows, but doesn't examine himself. He wants divine realization without making a human effort; he requires grace, yet makes demands; he wants to reap the wheat of truth without participating in the sowing; he hopes for peace of mind through faith without taking part in constructive work; he values science without consulting his conscience; he prefers ease without accepting responsibility, and living in the whirlwind of continual social drinking, clinging to lower interests and the utmost satisfaction of the physical senses, he waits for spirit messages..."

We were amazed by the interesting conclusions of our instructor friend.

Vicente was again deeply impressed and asked:

"What does this man want after all?"

Aniceto smiled and replied:

"He himself would find that very difficult to answer. For us, Vicente, Dr. Fidelis is one of those infirm persons who have not yet decided to look for relief because of their excessive attachment to the physical senses."

46

Continuing to Learn

According to Aniceto's information, there was still more than an hour until the beginning of the Gospel lecture, which for the incarnates in attendance, was Mr. Bentes' responsibility. However, the activity of the spirit service had already become very intense.

To the human eye, thirty-five flesh and blood persons were gathered there, but on our plane the number of needy spirits was in excess of two hundred, because the group was now augmented by many spirits who comprised the troublemaking entourage of the majority of the learners gathered in attendance. A special area had been set aside for them; it seemed to me that it entailed increased security measures due to the fact that they had been more or less forced to come because they were accompanying those who were intentionally seeking spiritual help, but who were there without the prior approval of the spirit guides working the public streets.

The activity was extensive and there was little time for any mere observation. All the workers of the house remained at their posts, paying the closest possible attention.

I noticed that on one corner of the large table there were numerous requests for *receituarios* and assistance. A wide variety of names were listed there. Many people had asked for medical advice, guidance, assistance and passes. Four spirit physicians were hard at work, and assisting their humanitarian efforts forty direct workers were coming and going, collecting information and adding to details.

We approached the great number of papers with names on them, and while I curiously sought to examine them, Aniceto explained:

"These are requests by people who state they are in need of immediate support and help."

"But do they receive everything they ask for?" asked Vicente curiously.

Our mentor smiled and replied:

"They receive what they need. Many ask for their bodies to be healed, but we are forced to consider to what extent this might be useful for them according to their individual desires; others request guidance of various types, obliging us to balance our work so as not to hinder individual freedom. Earthly existence is an active spiritual preparation course and almost always there is no lack of lazy students in the school, who waste time instead of making the most of it, and who are anxious for false achievements that require the least amount of effort. For this reason, in the area of guidance, the majority of the requests go unheeded. The request for therapy to maintain physical health by those who are actually interested in spiritual cooperation is always justified; nevertheless, as far as advice for daily living, great caution is essential on our part regarding the requests of those who intentionally disregard the obligation of Christian conduct. The Gospel is filled with sacred spiritual instructions, and disciples, at least before their own conscience, should consider themselves obliged to become familiar with them."

Our instructor friend took a short pause and changed his tone of voice as if to accentuate his words more strongly, and commented:

"It is possible that you will object and say that every question demands an answer and every request deserves a solution; however, in the case of answering certain requests by our incarnate fellow spirits, we must often resort to silence. How are we to recommend humility to those who preach it to others? How are we to teach patience to those who suggest it to their fellows, and how can we recommend the balm of work to those who are already able to condemn the laziness of others? Wouldn't this go against common sense? To read the rules of life to the blind and uneducated is a worthy task, but to repeat them to those who are already fully informed, wouldn't that be to underestimate the value of our time? Within the various denominations of Christianity, no soul receives Jesus' news for no apparent reason. So if every edifying work condition expresses the individual's commitment, then all knowledge of Christ implies responsibility. All disciples of the Master, therefore, have the duty to examine their conscience and bestow upon it insights based on Gospel precepts."

Vicente was listening with great interest and remarked:

"Nevertheless, one should venture to remember the ones who make similar requests frivolously..."

"Yes," Aniceto elucidated, smiling, "but we should not copy their impulses. Discarnates and incarnates who still misuse the possibilities of an exchange between the visible and invisible spheres for the ordinary person will pay a high price for their carelessness."

"In that case," I asked respectfully, "how do we respond to requests for guidance?"

"On rare occasions," explained our guide, "we will provide verbal assistance in answer to certain requests if they merit it and happen to have a bearing on spiritual matters, and if we can do so; nevertheless, it is almost always essential to answer nothing in a direct way, helping them silently. This is simply because we don't have a lot of time to remind our incarnate brothers and sisters of certain obligations that, for the sake of their own happiness, should not escape their memories."

Our kindly instructor was quiet for a few moments and then, wishing to clear up any doubts, he continued:

"Many discarnate spirits enjoy giving uninformed advice about various earthly situations and problems, but these poor friends hold themselves back in secondary issues and are incapable of a higher vision regarding the infinite horizons of eternal life. They turn themselves into mere slaves of the lower mentalities incarnated on the earth. They forget that our immediate interest right now must be, above all others, whatever relates to higher spirituality. Our disturbed brothers and sisters who offer uninformed advice to lazy incarnate minds about matters regarding humankind's just and necessary responsibilities must do so at their own expense."

"What happens, then?" asked Vicente curiously.

Our mentor, however, replied with another question:

"What happens to responsible people when they decide to spend time on aimless activities?"

At that moment, one of the spirit clinicians approached and was amiably greeted by Aniceto, who said to him after introducing us:

"Feel free to use our humble services. We're here as itinerant doctors, ready for active duty."

"Do you come from Nosso Lar?" asked our new friend, respectfully.

"Yes," replied Aniceto caringly.

"Very well," he said. "If possible, after the meeting I would like your help on two urgent cases. One is a young woman who discarnated today and the other is a dying man, my friend."

"But of course," stressed our guide solicitously." We'll await your instructions."

47

Hard at Work – Again

Bentes' interpretation of the Gospel, under the inspiration of an emissary of honorable position present at the gathering, was received with overall respect among the discarnate spirits.

There was not a similar display of harmony within the group of incarnates, however. A considerable instability of thought could be detected, and the anxious expectations of those present disturbed the vibratory current. Every now and then we were caught unawares by certain imbalances, which particularly affected the mediumistic abilities of Dona Isabel and the receptive attitude of the commentator, who seemed to lose his "train of thought," as is commonly said. Coworkers acted to reestablish the rhythm as far as possible. We noticed, though, that a few of the incarnate brothers and sisters were still extremely restless, especially the ones newest to the doctrinal knowledge, and who were acting very irresponsibly. Their minds were wandering very far from the uplifting commentaries. Their mental pictures could be seen clearly. Some of them were entangled in domestic matters, whereas others were impatient because they had not immediately achieved the goals that had brought them here.

Aniceto, who never missed the opportunity to explain something new, discreetly commented:

"Many disciples of Spiritism are concerned about the issue of concentration during work of a spiritual nature. There are many who set the standard regarding the outward appearance of the person who is concentrating. They are the ones who require a certain body posture, and who expect to see immediate results in activities of this sort. Nevertheless, those who say they are concentrating are of course referring literally to the 'act of gathering something together.' Well, if these incarnate friends don't take their responsibilities seriously outside the room of Spiritist practice, if they are perhaps cultivators of frivolity, indifference, deliberate and incessant error and stubbornness, and if they disregard the advice about perfection they give to others, what will they be able to 'gather together' during a few fleeting moments of spiritual endeavor? Good concentration requires a righteous life. So that our thoughts can be 'gathered together' in order to provide us with the ability for a noble union with the good, preparatory work involving mental meditative activities of a higher order is essential. An inner attitude of laxity toward the Gospel lessons they receive cannot instill believers or coworkers with a concentration of spiritual energies for spiritually constructive work just because they devote themselves for only a few minutes during the week to the thoughts of Christian love required of them. As you can see, this is a complex subject and demands at-length reflection and instruction."

I began to pay more attention to the incarnate bystanders. If it were not for the devotion of the coworkers on our plane, any tangible progress would have been impossible.

Isidoro and other devoted friends were hard at work, awakening some of the drowsy ones and readjusting the thoughts of the inattentive ones in order to neutralize certain harmful influences.

I realized that the immediate benefits of what Bentes was teaching were much more evident among the discarnates. In that group, there was not a single one who didn't garner direct consolation and sublime comfort.

Just as Bentes finished his commentary and before Dona Isabel went to devote herself to the *receituario* work, I saw a discarnate woman approach Isidoro and ask him emotionally:

"My brother, would it be possible to ask our guides on my behalf to see if I might communicate directly with my daughter? She's here at the meeting. I'm sure that, with due permission, our Isabel would heed my maternal anguish."

Isidoro showed a sincere desire to be helpful, but after exchanging a few words with a higher level instructor at the meeting, who was standing between the medium and Bentes, he answered her somewhat uncomfortably. His answer came as a great surprise to me:

"My sister," he said, "our esteemed Anselmo does not consider your request possible. He has informed me that your daughter is still not in any condition to receive such a blessing. For the time being, she needs to display what she learned from your example while you were incarnate, and she also needs to remain in the arena of opportunity without having to rely on you so heavily."

The woman was downcast, so Isidoro continued in a fraternal tone:

"But that's not the only reason Anselmo felt he had to turn you down. Such a measure would cause your maternal sentiments serious trouble. In her current evolutionary state, and taking old acquired habits into consideration, your daughter would depend too much on your aid. She would become too attached to her affectionate and sensitive mom, and you might find yourself disturbed in your new career as a spirit. She needs to be freer to display what she learned from your example, whereas your heart must remain free because of the worthy merit you achieved at the cost of your sweat and tears while on earth. Therefore, considering the sacred character of maternal love, our guides cannot grant your daughter the right to disturb you. Do you understand? Don't let this temporary impossibility upset you. Remember that we are all children of God. The Lord will provide means to help your daughter on your behalf. As for the rest, let us rejoice in our work. Keep in mind that although you will not be able to help her directly, we can resort to an indirect method. Who knows? Perhaps tomorrow you will be able to meet with your daughter in a dream."

The woman smiled, comforted, and replied:

"That's true. I must understand my new situation here."

At that moment, a spirit friend approached Isidoro with a request:

"My friend, I would appreciate your help with the physicians so they can provide additional recommendations for my nephew Amaro. He needs relief for his physical health."

Isabel's spirit husband displayed a meaningful expression and responded:

"I cannot, my friend, I cannot. If Amaro himself asks and the physicians agree, everything will be just fine; however, you are not unaware of the fact that our patient is very rebellious. I have already arranged to get him medical guidance from our plane five times, but he never acknowledged our efforts. He is not willing to buy the recommended medications, but whenever his friends do so for him, he disregards the dosing schedules and thinks he is above the method. He caustically criticizes the recommendations he receives and then makes use of them with disdain. Of course, I'm not annoyed by this, just as an adult would not be irritated by the games of a child; however, you must understand that we are dealing with a very sacred material and there is no time to waste on those who enjoy playing games. Furthermore, the act of giving to those who do not want to receive would not be charitable."

Isidoro spoke with an inflection of fraternal goodness, which smoothed over any sense of harsh frankness. I understood that to assist so many people and wend one's way through so many different matters, it would not be possible to treat them in any other way.

The work continued with great educational value for Vicente and me. The efforts of the spirit clinicians, along with the selflessness of the special intermediary, touched my heart. In fact, great self-denial was necessary to attend to the massive and considerable work in the area of assistance to the incarnates there because few attendees of the group seemed to maintain a corresponding attitude of sublime fraternal dedication in the name of the Master.

However, Aniceto, reading my thoughts, spoke kindly:

"Someday, Andre, you will understand with Jesus that it is better to serve than to be served; more blessed to give than to receive."

48

The Dread of Death

Our guide's many explanations answered my natural questions; nevertheless, there was still more to learn. Why were so many discarnates gathered there? Since they had already received spiritual assistance, couldn't they congregate in places that were just as spiritual on our plane?

I respectfully asked Aniceto about this.

"In fact, Andre," responded our generous mentor, "most of the discarnates receive invaluable instruction in our sphere of action. At the beginning of your new spirit experience, you yourself were not led to our corporeal friends' environment for the guidance you needed.

However, when they arrive here, a great number of individuals feel possessed by an unhealthy longing for groups of their own kind, as happens on other planes of evolution with animals when they feel a mortal longing for the herd. To strengthen the ability of such discarnates to adapt to their new 'habitat,' the rescue service is more effective when in close proximity to the magnetic energies of brothers and sisters who are still involved in the carnal circles. At moments like these, this room serves as a large incubator of psychic energies for the work of acclimating certain spirit bodies to the new life."

And pointing to a large assembly of needy spirits, he continued:

"The brothers and sisters in the situation I am referring to hear our voices and are indeed consoled by our aid, but human warmth is filled with magnetism of a more meaningful level for them. Upon such contact, they experience the awakening of new energies. That is why our cooperative work in centers of this sort offers advantages that you, for now, could not imagine. Didn't you see the lazy, drowsy and careless incarnates who came to receive benefits in this house? They, themselves, also gave something of themselves ... they gave magnetic warmth, beneficial vital emanations to this home sanctuary's benefactors who manipulate elements of this nature, distributing them in valuable fluid combinations to enfeebled and maladjusted spirits."

And, smiling, he concluded kindly:

"Everything has some value, Andre. Our Father has created nothing in vain."

When the meeting had ended with all-round benefits that I won't venture to describe in detail, Aniceto assisted a physician who wished to take advantage of his generous examination of his patients.

"Very often," exclaimed this physician from Dona Isabel's group, as if offering information to Vicente and me, "we not only administer medicine to infirm bodies, but we also guide discarnates who, during the course of their illnesses, had been under our care."

"Are there always many of them?" I asked.

"A growing number," he explained attentively. "There are occasions when we enjoy the cooperation of the patients' spirit friends or relatives, but in most cases we are forced to act by ourselves. Fortunately, we almost never lack dedicated and active helpers. There are fellow spirits who are devoted to caring for tubercular, blind, lame, leprous, disturbed and dying individuals by themselves. They are our dedicated coworkers in all sorts of situations."

We left the premises and in a few minutes we stopped in front of a huge building.

Our colleague kindly led us inside a spacious morgue, where we were faced with an interesting scene. The body of a young woman less than 30 years old was laid out, icy cold and stiff, with a male spirit at her side, watching over her. I was astonished to notice that the discarnate spirit was still attached to her remains. She seemed withdrawn into herself, harboring a strong feeling of fear. She shut her eyes deliberately, afraid of looking around her.

"The process of her disengagement from her physiological ties has ended," exclaimed the attentive physician, "but the poor thing has been overcome by a terrible feeling of dread for the last six hours."

And pointing to the spirit gentleman next to her, the physician explained:

"That is her fiancé. He has been waiting for her for a long time."

We moved a bit closer and heard him saying affectionately:

"Cremilda! Cremilda! Come along! Leave your tattered garment behind. I did everything possible so that you wouldn't suffer anymore ... Our little house is waiting for you, filled with love and light!..."

The young woman, however, closed her eyes as if she didn't want to see him. You could see perfectly well that her spirit body was completely detached from its physical vessel, but the poor thing remained stretched out, imitating the position of her corpse, and overcome with extreme terror.

Aniceto seemed to understand everything in the blink of an eye and made a subtle sign to the discarnate fellow, who approached him deeply troubled.

"You must help her differently," said our guide resolutely. "I can see that the poor thing has not slept during her disengagement and seems frightened due to her lack of spiritual preparation. It's not a good idea for you to show yourself to her right now ... In spite of the love you feel for her, she cannot see you again without becoming terribly upset at this moment in which her mind is floating about aimlessly..."

"Yes," he pondered sadly. "I have been calling her for six hours nonstop, and I too have noticed her dread."

Aniceto replied, counseling him:

"A lack of religious preparation, my brother. She will sleep, however, and as soon as she has been able to rest a little, we will deliver her into your care. For now, it's better to keep some distance."

And accompanying the physician, who had helped the young woman spiritually during her final days, Aniceto approached the newly discarnate, speaking in a fatherly manner:

"Cremilda, let's get you some new treatment."

Hearing him, the girl opened her terrified eyes and exclaimed:

"Oh, doctor, thank God! What a terrible nightmare! I felt as if I were in the kingdom of the dead, listening to my long deceased fiancé calling me to eternity!"...

"There is no death, my daughter!" refuted Aniceto affectionately. "Believe in life, in life eternal; profound, victorious life!"

"Are you a new doctor?" she asked, comforted.

"Yes, I have been called to give you some magnetic-based treatments. It is essential that you sleep and rest."

"That's for sure," she replied in a moving manner. "I'm very tired, and I need to rest..."

In a low voice, our instructor asked us to help in an inner attitude of prayer, and after remaining silent for a few seconds, he administered energizing passes to her. The young woman fell asleep almost immediately.

Aniceto moved her, pulling her away from her remains with the loving care of a father, and calling her grateful fiancé, gently passed her to him.

"Now you can show her the way, my brother."

The young man thanked him with tears of joy, and I saw him volitate with his face glowing, carrying with him the sweet burden of his love.

Our mentor made an expressive gesture and said:

"Because of the natural goodness of her heart and deliberate cultivation of virtue, she will need no purgatorial trials. It's a pity, though, that her mind had no preparation through religious education. Soon she will be adapted to her new life, however. The good ones don't encounter insurmountable obstacles."

And perhaps desiring to consolidate and synthesize the lesson, he concluded:

"As you can see, the concept of death is useless to truly alleviate, heal or edify. What is needed is to spread the idea of the victorious life. Moreover, the Gospel has already taught us for centuries that God is not the God of the dead, but the Father of creatures who live forever."

49

The Divine Machine

Not many minutes had passed before we were at the side of a dying man, whose situation truly concerned the spirit clinician.

He was a gentleman around sixty years old, slowly wasting away with leukemia.

"He fell into a coma several days ago," explained the physician, "but we need stronger magnetic aid to facilitate his disengagement."

In his room, besides two discarnate women – the mother of the dying man and a close relative – incarnate family members were deeply distraught.

Our guide examined the sick man slowly and stated:

"There's nothing left but to help him with his final disengagement."

Then, Aniceto recommended that we observe the dying man attentively.

Concentrating with all my ability, I focused on this man who was ready to discarnate. I noticed in detail that his soul was slowly withdrawing through various points of his body. I was astonished at seeing that right in the center of his skull there was a point of dying light, a candelabrum fluttering softly in the wind. It filled the entire encephalic region, awakening in me a deep sense of awe.

"That light," said my instructor friend, "is the mind; we have no human concept to explain its exact purpose at present."

Noticing my surprise, Aniceto put his right hand on my forehead, transmitting a vigorous magnetic influx to me, and stressed:

"Notice the humanized divine machine, the sacred tabernacle that the Lord enabled to form on earth as the sublime temporary habitation of the spirit. Andre, you are not looking at an anatomical demonstration of earthly science, examining dead flesh and rigid muscles. Observe! The mortal eye would not be able to see what you are looking at right now. The microscope is also limited, despite the fact that it is a noble victory for limited human eyesight."

The magnetic help of our dear mentor had changed the scene and I was compelled to concentrate all my energies so that my awe would not interfere with my observation.

Though dim, the mental light had become sharper and the body of the dying man seemed to assume gigantic proportions, thereby offering a surprising spectacle to my eager eyes. His body now seemed to me a wonderful factory in its most intimate details. That scientific picture was simply astounding. I identified, in oversized proportions, the nine organ systems of the human machine: the skeleton, the musculature, the blood circulation system, the blood purification apparatus subsumed in the lungs and kidneys, the lymphatic system, the digestive mechanism, the nervous system, the hormonal glands and the sense organs. Such a histological display was different from anything I could have dreamed of in my work in medicine. The circulating blood looked like it was moving along life-giving canals of that little world of bones, flesh, water, and residue. Millions of microscopic organisms were coming and going in the current that was depleted of red corpuscles. I witnessed the passing of strange forms: tiny containers loaded with deadly bacteria. Larger particles of microbial flora were being transformed into tiny boats accommodating miniscule beasts of prey by the hundreds. They were invading all the body's cellular nuclei. The organs, such as the lungs, liver and kidneys, were being irreparably assaulted by an incalculable number of infinitesimal saboteurs. And as the invading microbes were consolidating in certain cellular areas, something slowly began to stand out in the region under attack – a new form was being expelled from the worn out and aging one. In this way, I realized that discarnation was occurring via a gradual process. It was a valuable lesson. I noticed that some of the glands were making a desperate effort to send certain amounts of hormones to the invaded areas, but they were immediately absorbed by the deadly particles. The blood plasma appeared to be a strange gangrenous liquid.

I saw from the excessive movement of the mental wave that the dying man was trying to regain control of his bodily processes, but to no avail. All the cellular complexes were struggling against one another and the bacteria seemed to be enjoying their right to increasing and festive multiplication.

"Do you see the divine machine, formed by a preexisting spirit mold?" asked Aniceto, understanding my profound wonder. "The body of an incarnate human being is a tabernacle and a blessing. From this distressing extinction of an existence, you can see that all the movements of the body are subordinate to the managerial processes of the mind. The living body, Andre, represents a laborious conquest of earthly humanity on the Eternal Father's roster of bestowals. You can now identify the movements of living matter. Each organ is an autonomous department in the cellular realm, but subordinate to the individual's thoughts. Each gland is a center of active service. There is a great similarity between the human body and the modern machine. They both run on fuel with the difference that in humans chemical combustion obeys the spiritual sense that directs organic life. It is the mind that governs this wonderful factory. Our minds don't possess merely our character, reason, memory, direction, balance and understanding, but also the control of all the phenomena of corporeal expression. In the mental seat, and consequently in the brain, are all the distribution records of the vital principles for the cellular nuclei, including water and sugar. The metabolic centers are large workshops of incessant activity. The human mind, although indefinable by limited scientific earthly concepts, is the center of all manifestations of life on the planet. Each organ, each gland, my friend, plays a part in the work of the sublime machine that has been constructed in the subtle mold of the preexisting spirit body, and precisely for this reason, the day will come when science will recognize every human abuse as actually being self-inflicted harm. The human factory is a repository of electrical energies of highly constructive or destructive potential. Each cell is a tiny engine running on mental impulse."

Aniceto became still for a few moments, and while I was looking awe-stricken at the strange microbial phenomena in the dying man's body, he resumed his instructive talk:

"Here we see a brother at the moment of his disengagement. Notice his inability to control his conflicted cells. His bloodstream has been transformed into a channel for deadly invaders, which have not run into any defensive fortifications. You can observe and identify millions of units of tuberculosis, leprosy, diphtheria and cancer, which until now had been contained in the cellar of his physiological activity by an organized defense, but which have now multiplied alarmingly, on a par with other microbes as prolific as they are terrible. Nutrition has been interrupted. There is no possibility of new hormonal supplies. The dying man is withdrawing bit by bit, but still has not totally abandoned his flesh, because of a lack of mental education. This can be noticed in the excessive intemperance of the cells, over which he does not even have partial control. It is obvious that this man lived a life far removed from self-discipline. His physiological elements are too impulsive, obeying instinct much more than concentrated reason. To tell you the truth, our friend here is not discarnating; he is being expelled from the divine machine, where – from what we can see – it seems he did not fully appreciate the sublime gifts of God."

50

Fernando's Discarnation

When Aniceto removed his right hand from my forehead, I was no longer able to continue my observations of the infinitesimal. My vision included details very important to the general interest; however, I was nowhere close to that power of understanding that my mentor friend had transmitted to me by the touch of his elevated magnetic power.

Concentrating my visual energies, I continued to analyze the bone structure, the blood, tissues and humors, but the microscopic combat had disappeared as if by magic. In any case, however, I was greatly surprised as I now realized my X-ray potentiality.

After offering the same instructions to Vicente, Aniceto got involved in something new.

In the man's room was a group of grieving relatives. An incarnate doctor was carefully examining the dying man.

At that moment, two spirits, who were in the room and who had given us only the usual greetings, approached our instructor and asked him to take more forceful action.

"Please, noble friend," said the woman who had been the dying man's mother, "help us remove my poor son from his wasted body. We have been waiting many hours for someone who could help us in our predicament. I have tried to comfort him but it's been no use!" emphasized the dignified woman mournfully. "He continues in a state of dolorous and terrible incomprehension. He is completely imprisoned by the sensations of physical suffering, just as he was tied to the satisfactions of the body during the course of his existence."

Aniceto agreed, adding:

"In fact, you can notice great gaps in the dying man's mental expression. It's clear that he spent his human life obeying instinct more than reason. Large indications of how undisciplined he was can be observed in his cellular makeup. We might help him disentangle himself from his strongest ties to the physical realm, however."

"That would indeed be a kind favor," replied the distressed mother.

"Have you been given the responsibility of taking him?" asked our instructor, comprehending the magnitude of the task. "We should consider this because it will take only a few minutes for full disengagement to occur."

She gestured sadly and replied:

"I would like to sacrifice myself a bit further for my unfortunate Fernando, but I obtained permission only to help him in his final moments. My superiors promised to help him, but advised me to leave him alone for awhile. Fernando needs to reconsider his past and recognize the values he unfortunately disdained. Tears and remorse in the solitude of repentance will be the bearers of calm to his unreasoning spirit. My desire to nestle him close to my heart, returning to times gone by, is great; nevertheless, I cannot jeopardize the forward progress of divine learning with my maternal tenderness. Fernando truly is the child of my affections; however, both he and I have accounts to settle with Eternal Justice, and as for me, I am tired of running deeper into debt. I must not contest the designs of God."

At this point in the dialog, the spirit clinician who had sent us there interrupted, politely informing us:

"Our friend is right. Fernando will not be able to leave with her, but her maternal intercession has been so noteworthy that I have instructions to take him to a safe place, a rescue home, where he will be able to glean the most advantage from his suffering, since he will be sheltered in a vibratory zone that is inaccessible to inferior and criminal influences, even though it is located in the lower regions."

"Yes, I know," murmured Aniceto in a grave tone. "That is a very prudent move."

Then as someone who had no time to lose, he asserted:

"The distress of his incarnate relatives here could cause us problems in doing this. Notice how all of them are emitting magnetic aid to benefit the dying man."

Indeed, a network of grayish and dimly illuminated strands seemed to link the relatives to the nearly dead patient.

"Such aid," said Aniceto, "is useless now to give him back his organic balance. We need to neutralize these energies, as they are being emitted out of distress, and above all, we must provide peace of mind to the family."

And moving even closer to the sufferer, he assumed the posture of a magnetizer, and declared:

"Let's modify the status of the coma."

After a few minutes of our mentor's efforts, supported by our respectful silence, we heard the incarnate doctor announce to the relatives of the dying man:

"Well, his prognosis seems to have improved. Inexplicably, his pulse is almost normal and his breathing is normalizing."

The three women gave a sigh of relief.

"Dona Amanda," said the assistant to the dying man's wife, "it would be a good idea for you to go and rest a bit, and take your sisters-in-law with you. Fernando is very peaceful now and his situation is truly favorable. Mr. Januario and I will continue to watch over him."

The women, along with two gentlemen, who were getting ready to leave, offered contented and heartfelt thanks. The only ones who remained in the room were the doctor and one of the patient's brothers. His sudden improvement had set everyone more at ease. And bit by bit the grayish strands that had been attached to the patient disappeared without leaving a trace.

"Let's open the window," said the contented doctor. "Perhaps the air will help speed up our friend's improvement."

Mr. Januario complied, opening a wide windowpane.

I was deeply astonished at noticing that three horrible faces with diabolical expressions had suddenly appeared at the windowsill, and were asking in a loud voice:

"What's going on? Is Fernando coming or not?"

No one answered. I noticed, however, that Aniceto gave them a sobering look, and this gesture alone compelled them to disappear.

A half hour passed, during which the doctor and Mr. Januario, practically unconcerned about the dying man because of his improvement, had begun an animated conversation about the world's problems.

Aniceto took advantage of the peaceful atmosphere and began to remove Fernando's spirit body, disengaging it from the remains. I noticed that he had begun the operation from the heels, finishing at the head, to which the dying man seemed to be attached by a long cord, like that of a newborn child. Aniceto broke it forcefully. Fernando's body shuddered, calling the human doctor to the new situation. The process had been neither short nor easy. It had lasted several minutes, during which I saw our instructor use all the means of his concentration and perhaps of his magnetic energies.

Informed by Mr. Januario, the deceased's grieving family entered the room noisily.

The discarnate's mother, however, helped by Aniceto and the spirit physician who had brought us there, gave her son the assistance he needed. A few minutes later, while his earthly family kneeled sobbing over the corpse, the little expedition consisting of three spirits – the two women and the clinician – left, carrying the discarnate to the assistance institute. I noticed, however, that they didn't leave by means of volitation, but walked like ordinary mortals.

I was extremely impressed. I was especially intrigued by the appearance of those satanic faces when the window was opened. Why such contempt for a sufferer?

As we left the residence, our instructor looked at me attentively, and before I could formulate any question, he explained:

"Don't worry too much about those rogues waiting for our unfortunate brother, Andre. They were unable to enter the sickroom solely because the noble maternal presence prevented such an assault."

And after remaining silent for a few moments, he added:

"Each individual in life cultivates the affections he prefers. Fernando liked unruly companions, so it is not unusual that they came to wait for him at the time of his return to real existence. In Hebrews 12, Paul of Tarsus affirms that humans are surrounded by a great 'cloud of witnesses.' Well, this information was addressed to the human spirit nearly twenty centuries ago. Everyone, then, has the invisible entourage to which they are devoted on earth. Later on, when society learns the grandeur of the lessons of the Gospel, all people will be more careful in choosing their witnesses."

51

Saying Goodbye

After numerous other spirit activities, the week of service during which Aniceto had allowed us to accompany him came to an end.

We had followed our noble instructor through varied and complex tasks. Stationed at Isabel's inviting temple, we had assisted a considerable number of patients, as well as other disturbed, prostrated, corrupted and dying brothers and sisters. For all of the cases, our guide had improvised wonderful resources, and was always attentive and optimistic.

Those few days of new work had filled my mind with new thoughts and my heart with sentiments that I had not known before.

In contact with Aniceto's revelations within the domains of electricity and magnetism, all my former knowledge about medicine had been reformed. The mind's ascendancy in the body's equilibrium, its radioactive forces, the field of bacteria, a broader vision of organized matter, all compelled me to sustain a new scientific concept in the art of healing infirm bodies.

Above all, an understanding of the Divine Doctor, who restores the health of the immortal spirit, had developed in my soul. This extensive clarity, which now made my spirit rejoice, provided me with a deeper knowledge of Jesus. Thus, I understood that faith does not consist of an affirmation of the lips, nor of joining an established church. I had been searching for faith in vain in the sectarian sphere, in common arguments, in outward worship that changes every day. Yes, it was a fount of living water, giving birth spontaneously in my soul. It had been transformed into a profound reverence, allied to the highest concept of service and responsibility before the sublime bestowals of the eternal Father. I had found a treasure inaccessible to destruction and a non-transferable asset, which had been born and consolidated within me.

When our instructor invited us to return, I definitely felt like a different person. By discovering my own interior world, I had the impression of having received the news directly from the Lord Jesus.

How could I ever repay our esteemed Aniceto for such a capitalization of immortal assets?

A prayer service had ended the last weekly meeting at Isidoro and Isabel's home.

The ongoing work had been an arena of observations and experiences that were always new.

A large number of Aniceto's friends had gathered around the instructor, eager to share in the light of the conversation and the goodbyes.

Our devoted guide offered to everyone some words of encouragement, optimism, happiness and trust in the Lord like the prince in the legend whose mouth was an inexhaustible fountain of spiritual gold.

Vicente and I had moist eyes as we wished to express to him verbally our recognition of the blessings we had received, but as we approached him, our selfless guide smiled and said:

"Let's thank Jesus for everything he has given us."

And taking the Bible as if he wanted to focus the subject on the love of holy things, he read aloud from the second chapter of Solomon's Proverbs:

"My son, if you will accept my words, and keep my commandments so that you may incline your ear to wisdom, and apply your heart to understanding; if you clamor for understanding and lift up your voice for knowledge; if you will seek it as silver, and search for it as for hidden treasures, then you will understand the fear of the Lord and find the knowledge of God."[1]

[1]Proverbs 2:1-5 (Spirit author's note)

Then he placed the sacred book on the table and commented:

"Let us remember the Lord as we say farewell. Let us reaffirm our commitment to work and witness, my brothers and sisters. In this short passage from Proverbs we find many words of interest to Christian minds. To accept the divine commandments and keep them, to keep one's ear alert and one's heart enlightened, to ask for understanding and intelligence, lifting our voices above lower objectives, to seek the treasures of Christ and his program of services, these represent the noble effort of one who indeed desires divine wisdom. Let us not forget these duties."

Since our dear friend had taken a longer pause, a brother begged him to continue his interpretation of the text, but Aniceto replied in a fraternal tone:

"That won't be possible right now, my brother. Other obligations are calling us from far away."

And directing himself privately to Vicente and me, he added:

"Since we'll be returning by the ordinary road, we can wait for our friend Isabel to give her our thanks and goodbyes."

A few moments thereafter, Isidoro's noble companion, abandoning her body to the repose of sleep, came over to us with her spirit husband in answer to the mental invitation of our dedicated guide. Aniceto expressed his deep gratitude to her, spoke of our happiness and the holy opportunities for service that divine benevolence had given us.

Dona Isabel was moved and thanked him, showing the tears of gratitude that dominated her spirit.

"Noble Aniceto," she said, wiping her eyes, "please come back as often as possible to our humble home. Teach me patience and courage, my kind friend! When you can, don't let me stray from my motherly duties, which are so difficult to fulfill in the flesh, where less worthy interests violently collide. Support my obligations as a servant of the Gospel of our Lord! Deep longings for my spirit family have rent my heart at times ... I would like to transport my children to the higher spheres and incline them toward the good, so that our divine union on the higher planes of life is not delayed. Homesickness for Nosso Lar pierces my soul, at times threatening my humble work on earth. Noble Aniceto, don't forget your poor and imperfect friend. I know that Isidoro follows me step by step, but he and I need friends who are strong in the faith – like you – who revive our spirits on the journey of Christian duty!..."

Sister Isabel could not continue because the tears had choked her voice. Aniceto, with shining and serene eyes, embraced her like a father and spoke gently:

"Isabel, continue with your witnessing and don't be afraid. We will be with you, now and forever. Many admirable individuals have had duties, but let's not forget, my daughter, that Jesus experienced duty and sacrifice in the world. We shall not lack the tender care of our vigilant Guide on the road to redemption. Keep your spirits up and walk on!"

Then, looking directly at all of us, our noble friend exclaimed:

"Now, brothers and sisters, help me pray!"

And holding Isabel and Isidoro as one in his heart, Aniceto lifted his eyes and spoke with sublime beauty:

"Lord, teach us to receive the blessings of service! We still do not know, beloved Jesus, how to understand the extent of the work you have entrusted to us! Let us, Lord, be able to form the conviction in our soul that the work of the world belongs to you so that vanity will not insinuate itself into our hearts through the appearance of good!

Give us, Master, the spirit of consecration to our duties and unconcern for the results, which belong to your love!

Teach us to act without the fetters of the passions so that we may recognize your holy purposes!

Beloved Lord, help us to be your loyal servants;

Beloved Master, grant us your instruction;

Righteous Judge, lead us on straight paths;

Sublime Physician, restore our health;

Compassionate Pastor, lead us to the fount of living water;

Wise Engineer, give us your blueprint;

Magnanimous Administrator, inspire us in our tasks;

Sower of Good, teach us to cultivate the fields of our souls;

Divine Carpenter, help us to build our eternal home;

Careful Potter, patch the vessel of our heart;

Watchful Friend, be also tolerant of our weaknesses;

Prince of Peace, have compassion on our fragile spirits; open our eyes and show us the highway to your kingdom!"

Aniceto fell silent. With moist eyes that were finding it difficult to hold back their tears of gratitude, I joined the noble caravan that would be returning with us to Nosso Lar.